$\mathcal{U}$NLIKELY $\mathcal{H}$ERO

A DIEPPE SURVIVOR'S GIFT OF HOPE

ISBN 0-919939-44-9

Printed and bound in Canada by
The Aylmer Express Ltd.
March, 1997

DEDICATION

To Helen, June, and Victor

$\mathcal{A}$CKNOWLEDGEMENTS

Don (Donovan) Errey, in common with most who survived active service in World War II, was for many years reluctant to share the story of his experiences. We are indebted to him for the privilege, many years later of hearing this remarkable account, and grateful for his permission to publish these glimpses into the life of a remarkable survivor of Dieppe and Stalag 9C.

His acts of courage and fortitude, and his assistance in the rehabilitation of seriously wounded fellow prisoners exemplifies those qualities of the ordinary soldier which have made our country great.

Thanks go to Patti Squires, Christine Thorpe and Bruce McKim for their helpful suggestions.

We pay special tribute to the late Hugh Bremner, who assisted in the many hours spent interviewing and taping these reminiscences. Appreciation also to Elma DaCosta and Joyce Lee who typed the manuscript, and to Mary MacKenzie for her careful editing and proof reading.

George Kerr
Douglas MacKenzie
London, Ontario 1997

$\mathcal{I}$NTRODUCTION

Historians are fond of pointing out that Canadians are an unmilitary lot — slow to anger, not the least blood-thirsty, and totally lacking the bellicosity essential for warfare. Nevertheless, in less than a century, Canada spent fifteen years in battle — in South Africa, the two World Wars, and Korea. Wars are traumatic for combatants and non-combatants alike, and Canadians are understandably reluctant to be reminded of them, let alone to prepare for the next.

They were certainly reluctant in September 1939. There were few parades on the day Canada entered World War II — no cheering, tearful crowds, no massed renditions of Rule Britannia, no long lines at recruiting depots. All these had happened on August 14, 1914, from Victoria to Halifax, but then few knew what war meant. By 1918, with 60,000 of her youth dead in Europe, Canadians knew — and no one wanted the lesson repeated.

Canadian attitudes toward the military in the Thirties were shaped not only by the remembrance of the Great War but also by the grim realities of the Great Depression. A heavy cost had been paid for participation in European quarrels — too many were chasing too few jobs, to worry about Canada's defences. Let the European dictators begin again to redraw the map of Europe; this would no longer be a concern for Canadians. The attitude was rejection of conflict, if not outright pacifism.

Canadian shores in the Thirties were guarded by a tiny navy and an almost non-existent air force. As for the army — the Permanent Army and Non-Permanent Active Militia together could muster fewer than 55,000 officers and men. This, then, was the protection for a nation of over eight million people and a territory of nearly four million square miles.

Equipment? Obsolete, what there was of it. A. W. McNaughton,

Chief of the General Staff, reported in 1935 that stocks of ammunition for the remaining World War I field pieces represented only 90 minutes' fire at normal rates. There were no modern anti-aircraft guns, and the guns of the coastal defence artillery had not been tested in years for want of ammunition.

Then war became certain, and conditions slowly improved. Parliament appropriated funds for material, in particular for the Air Force. Government relief programs directed large numbers of workers into construction of barracks, armouries, training facilities.

Still, Canada entered the conflict in September 1939 woefully unprepared. With equipment in short supply, with war aims yet undefined, with the situation in Europe largely unknown, the first volunteers for military service were true pioneers, and their act of enlistment an adventure. It was a costly one. Vacillation and bungling at the top led to frustration, boredom, misdirected effort, and frequently to death.

Yet, for all that, it remained for many a great adventure, an experience which affected the rest of their lives, for good or ill. Unfortunately few accounts exist of the experiences of individual Canadians in World War II. There has been a flood of memoirs from German Air Aces, American infantrymen, British sailors and generals and politicians of all nationalities. And most of the warring nations, including Canada, have produced official histories , replete with dry accumulations of unit numbers and logistics figures, decorated with beflagged maps of campaigns and battles. But the story of individual Canadians, especially those of the Rank and File — the privates and corporals — is nearly non-existent.

Although their experience is not unique as participants in a great adventure shared by thousands, they were affected nonetheless in ways only they could understand or express. This is the story of one ordinary Canadian soldier, a member of the Rank and File, who participated in that most grievous of Canadian military tragedies, Dieppe. It includes participation in the short-lived Canadian Commando - the Vikings, long years of imprisonment as a Prisoner of War (POW), made bearable through daring, if occasionally humourous, escape attempts and acts of sabotage. Finally it portrays the life of a man whose unchanneled energies, which so often found destructive outlets, were gradually redirected in purpose and meaning toward an humanitarian goal. In a small workshop inside Stalag 9C he created and built artificial limbs for hundreds of Allied Amputees, and gave their lives new hope.

CHAPTER ONE

In the late Thirties in the small Ontario town of Wallaceburg, close to the United States border, the place to see and be seen for the high school crowd was "Pop" Gurd's restaurant. The corner juke box, that magic carpet of adolescent fantasies, was rarely still, and banana splits were a house speciality at fifteen cents. Don Errey and Angus MacKenzie were regulars, who liked to engage "Pop" in his favorite topic of conversation — the Detroit Tigers — and as avid and polite listeners, could usually count on at least one free "rock-n-rye" cola. It was during yet another recounting of Pop's favorite story — the exploits of Tiger great Ty Cobb — that the desultory life of his teenage listeners came to an end. Pop stopped in mid-sentence. He reached for the volume knob on his Rogers Majestic radio. A special news bulletin from radio station WJR in Detroit reported that Britain had officially declared war on Germany for violating Poland's neutrality. It was September 3, 1939.

War in Europe was inevitable, especially after the Russo-German pact in mid-August. But it was all very far away from Wallaceburg. The baseball season was winding down, the struggling Tigers were in fifth place, 16 games behind the mighty Yankees. It was harvest time, and the boys were looking forward to another lazy Canadian autumn. What had Danzig and the Polish Corridor to do with a couple of teenagers thousands of miles from Europe? The boys had been vaguely aware that they would perhaps have to get into uniforms in the near future. The special news broadcast made things clear. Both of them would be in battle dress before the month ended. Don was 17; Angus had just turned 16.

Not that they knew nothing of war: the conversations over ice cream and ginger ale in Gurd's that summer were all about war — the last one. Many older inhabitants of Wallaceburg and neighbouring Chatham, of Dresden and Thamesville, as well as of the metropolis, Windsor, had served in the regiments of the Canadian Expeditionary Force, and memories of "the war to end all wars" were still vivid. The local regiments, the Kent Militia and the Essex Scottish, had fought in France and Belgium, and, like all Canadian regiments, had suffered heavy casualties. No one knew what a future war would be like, but imagined it would be no better than the last one.

There was little doubt, now that Britain had officially entered the War, that Canada, the senior dominion of the British Commonwealth, would quickly follow. Two sons of Lord Tweedsmuir, then Governor-General of Canada, immediately enlisted in the Canadian Forces. But for the first time in its history, Canada would exercise that prerogative of independent nationhood, a declaration of War, at its own discretion.

On September 10, 1939, the Hon. Vincent Massey, Canada's High Commissioner to Britain, received a cablegram from the Department of External Affairs at Ottawa. He copied it in longhand on two pieces of foolscap paper and immediately presented it to the King. As reported in the London (Ontario) Free Press these two ordinary sheets, one of which is inscribed "approved George R.I.", bear the official declaration that a state of war existed between Canada and Germany. George VI as King of the United Kingdom was at war with Germany on September 3, 1939. George VI as King of Canada entered the war on September 10.

The one-week delay served to remind the rest of the world of Canada's independent status. It was also a week of considerable reflection for thousands of Canadians as they pondered a life in uniform. On September 9th Don made his decision. He would enlist. Immediately he set off to discuss plans with Angus, who was busy contemplating the merits of cutting the family lawn. The two boys sat in the shade of a maple tree and talked about joining up. They were both under the legal enlistment age, but that problem could be faced later. Their real concern was that the army might run out of uniforms before they got to the recruiting depot.

"Let's go, Angus," said Don finally, and they walked to the main road, leaving the lawnmower unattended, the grass uncut.

They hitched a ride into Chatham and went to the Kent regiment's depot. They were too early; the regiment had not yet geared up for mobilization. The two would-be soldiers had not acquired any regimental loyalty, perhaps the Essex Scottish would take them.

The Essex Scottish presented no problem, at least not for Angus, who was accepted at once. Don, a year older, had a hard time persuading the recruiting sergeant that he was of military age, which he wasn't, but if Angus could get in so should he.

"All right, fellows," said the sergeant at last. "Fall in tomorrow at 8 a.m. sharp. Just bring your tooth-brush. The army supplies everything else."

Back home, it was tougher trying to convince their parents that their actions had been wise. Their argument, that failure to report would lead to court-martial and jail, failed to impress. However, knowing the boys were feeling their oats and not wishing to dampen their enthusiasm, the parents agreed. Both boys were underage, they reasoned, and once the army knew, they would surely be sent home.

Next morning, swaggering slightly, Don and Angus said their good-byes and climbed on the bus. Arriving in Windsor, they were directed to the Marketorium, on Ouellette Avenue, a long, four-storey building which the army had requisitioned as a holding area for new recruits.

The boys were ushered into the building to help themselves to breakfast. Instead of the hardtack and bully beef they had been led to expect by Old Sweats from the last war, they found quantities of sandwiches, buns, custard pies, cakes, and gallons of coffee.

"Hey, Angus, the army's going to be just fine if we eat like this all the time, eh?"

As they were to discover later the army didn't know what to do with the flood of new recruits, beyond keeping them fed. After eating, they waited. When nothing happened, they ate some more, and waited some more. At last, a sergeant in full uniform appeared and assigned them to billets in town. First, lots of grub, and now sheets and blankets on a soft bed in a civilian home. This wasn't the army they had heard about!

The pattern of eat and wait, eat and wait was repeated the next day. At 4 p.m. they were finally ordered to fall in. Each man was then signed up as a private in the Essex Scottish regiment, and sworn into the army. They were soldiers at last — or so they thought. But even the least perceptive of the new men realized that he would have a long way to go before he could earn a rightful place in the regiment.

Don and Angus' knowledge of their new regiment was sketchy at best. They would learn that the Essex Scottish was one of Canada's oldest regiments. It traced its history back to the Detroit militia in 1763, when the area across the Detroit River was still British territory. The militia of Essex County took part in the war of 1812, and were called to arms on the outbreak of the rebellion in Upper Canada in 1837. In 1885, the Essex Militia became the 21st Essex Battalion of Infantry, and two years later, the 21st Battalion, Essex Fusiliers. A draft from the regiment was sent to South Africa in 1900 as part of the Canadian Volunteer Force fighting the Boers, and the regiment participated in the major battles involving the Canadian Expeditionary Force in the First World War. In 1927, the regiment was renamed the Essex Scottish (Highlanders), adopted Highland uniforms, and completed the Scottish theme by choosing "Highland Laddie" as its regimental march. Despite stringencies imposed by the parsimonious policies of successive Canadian governments, the Essex Scottish continued as one of the most active militia units between the wars, winning the Infantry Association Cup for smartness and efficiency eight times between 1927 and 1939.

The dress uniform of the Essex Scottish is an important factor in the regiment's tradition, and following the swearing-in ceremonies the new recruits were taken to the Windsor Armouries to receive their kit. Don looked forward to his future transformation in the spectacular Highland uniform of the regiment: the red and green McGregor tartan kilt and tie, tailored tunic, Glengarry cap.

"Sorry, boys," said the Quartermaster-Sergeant. "This is all we got." What was in the store was scarcely enough to clothe a corporal's guard, much less several hundred new recruits.

When they had put on what had been given them, Don and Angus looked like slightly more belligerent civilians. The more fortunate had acquired World War I tunics with shiny brass buttons, but that was all. No kilts, no Glengarries, not even boots, the infantry's essential item. Don and Angus stared at each other, then at their fellow Highland warriors. Each held a Lee-Enfield rifle, left over from the previous hostilities, which was tipped by a long, evil-looking sword bayonet of the same vintage. Wrapped around each waist was a broad web belt with bayonet scabbard, set off by incongruous civilian flannels or dungarees. The regular militiamen, very spit-and-polish, bustled around the ragtag assembly, conscious that they were the real soldiers, with the uniforms to prove it.

Despite their unmartial appearance, the new recruits did their best to act like soldiers, with parades, drills and fatigues around the Marketorium. If nothing else, they at least had enthusiasm, and a growing notion of what military discipline meant.

For several weeks, they paraded at the Armouries, knocking off at the unmilitary hour of 3 p.m.. Parts of uniforms trickled in, one item at a time, tunics, hose, caps, kilts. As in every army, Canadian soldiers' uniforms came in the regulation sizes of too large and too small. Don, on the diminutive side, got one which fit him like a bell tent. But he wasn't about to pass it up in hopes of finding a better fit later. He took it to a civilian tailor, who cut a proper fit for a large chunk of army pay. Don now lacked only boots. He wore his civilian shoes and so had to be excused from drill. The army's shortage of boots was so chronic in those early days that footgear was inspected on parade each morning. Possessors of wafer-thin soles were excused further marching and square-bashing until they were properly shod.

As autumn gave way to winter, the constant drill and the arrival of their boots gave the raw recruits at least the appearance of soldiers. Packs, kitbags, more rifles, webbing — the supplies began to pour in as the Canadian war effort finally got into gear. The Essex Scottish also moved out of civilian billets and into the military, and far less civilized, surroundings of St. Luke's Barracks in Walkerville.

While the Essex Scottish in 1939 was hardly ready to terrify the Wehrmacht, the regiment did arouse the curiosity of the Americans. Detroit was just across the river, and Americans poured through the tunnel to see such exotic sights as the Essex Scottish changing the guard, and fierce-looking kilted warriors slapping rifles around in an almost professional arms drill.

Some of these Americans stayed to join the Canadian forces: some seeking adventure, some for less worthy reasons. The Canadian army at this time offered a haven to many Americans in trouble with the law. Don went out one night to the Market to meet with a new acquaintance, a casual American friend, who wanted to be seen with the brave Canadian lads in uniform. As Don approached the Market, he saw a crowd and a lot of policemen asking questions. Then he saw the body of his friend lying in a pool of blood. He had been machine-gunned to death. Bystanders said that the man had been a member of Detroit's underworld and had met the fate usually faced by those who double-crossed the mob. Don kept on walking back to the safety of the barracks.

The traffic sometimes went the other way: several Canadian soldiers deserted and looked for sanctuary on the other side of the border. Border guards and customs officials were always suspicious of Canadians in uniform, presumably on the theory that deserters always walked about in their battledress or kilts.

One evening a few of Don's friends from Wallaceburg showed up at the barracks, and suggested that they visit some MacKenzie relatives in Detroit. Angus and Don had passes that night, so they piled into the car, pulling on their friends' coats over their uniforms, and jamming borrowed Homburgs over their short military haircuts. All went well at first. They went through the tunnel to Detroit and stopped at the U.S. Customs post. The guard asked the usual questions:

"Where you fellows from? How long you gonna stay in Detroit? Anything to declare?

Cigarettes? Liquor?"

He looked at Don and Angus in the back seat, who smiled angelically back at him. Suddenly he sprang to the door and pulled it open. Looking down, he saw four brilliantly blancoed spats.

"OK, you two, out of the car, and come with me. The rest of you can go."

Back in the Customs post, the two "deserters" were fingerprinted, handcuffed, and led back to the Canadian side. The Customs man was jovial as he unlocked the cuffs.

"Sorry, fellows, but as long as the States is neutral you can't come over in uniform. You'll just have to stay on your side of the line."

Don and Angus jovially shook hands with the customs officer and left. They had a plan. Back in Windsor, they hopped on a bus which carried them via the Ambassador Bridge, through a different Customs post, and into Detroit. There they joined up with their friends again and went on a tour of Detroit's taverns.

In full uniform, the recruits were a hit in American border towns. Before the war, the militiamen had often paraded with the regimental pipe band through the streets of Port Huron and Detroit. Now that Canada was at war, the raw would-be soldiers were an exotic species to the still officially neutral Americans. It was the kilt that did it, of course. Most of the men took care to wear something under it, as much to ward off the effects of below-zero cold as to maintain respectability in the winds blowing off Lake St. Clair. One of Don's friends, Reg Sherwood, preferred to maintain his lower depths in a state of freedom, unencumbered by BVDS or scratchy Stanfields. He was immensely popular in the bars of Port Huron, hitching the kilt up a little higher with each round bought by the locals.

While many of the Americans in the Essex Scottish were on the run from their wives or the law, others were simply seeking the adventure of war in faraway places. One was an eighteen-year-old whom the men at first dubbed Little Lord Fauntleroy. He was James Palms, son of a prominent theatre owner in Detroit. Out riding one day, he simply left his horse, crossed the border, jumped on a bus, and showed up at the Armouries still wearing full riding habit. No questions were asked; Palms took the oath like all other Americans in the Essex Scottish. It wasn't until many months later, after the regiment had moved to Camp Borden, that private detectives hired by his parents caught up with the escapee. He refused to return, and his parents forgave him, especially when he qualified for a commission as a second lieutenant. Palms became a good officer. Along with a hundred others in the regiment, he later died on the beach at Dieppe.

Don was quickly caught up in an active social life in Windsor, even though he had to be back in barracks every night. At one time he was dating an engaging young lady, and making certain rather unscrupulous plans for her. Then he met her brother, a champion boxer whose friendly advice to his sister's kilted swain was, "Lay one finger on her, mister, and I'll tear you in half." The romance cooled with the weather. Winter descended on Windsor; the Detroit River froze; snow lay piled everywhere; the wind blew through every crack in the barracks walls. Don found that the kilt was no garment to be wearing in a Canadian winter. Even Sherwood finally gave in and wore drawers. On one particularly cold night, as Don piled wood into the makeshift brazier which served to warm those on guard duty outside the barracks, he accidentally set the sentry box on fire. Worse followed on New Year's Eve, one of the

Don Errey in the dress uniform of the Essex Scottish.

coldest in memory in the Windsor area. With burlap wrapped around his bare knees, kilt flapping against his legs, and a cruel draft chilling his nether regions, Don slowly paced his guard area. Imperceptibly, the cold crept through, until Don found his legs seized up solid, like rusted machinery. The military mind is quick to react in such emergencies. Without pausing to shout for help, Don loosed off the blank cartridge in his rifle. Men poured out of the barracks, ready for anything. Now Don found his voice: "I'm bloody froze!" The military machine moved into action. Rescuers picked him up, carried him into the barracks like a slab of frozen beef, dropped him on his cot, and mumbling dark oaths went back to sleep.

No matter what the weather, the routine of drill, physical training and hikes continued. The men learned elementary fieldcraft in Yawkey bush on the outskirts of Windsor. It was, as Don said, "amateurish — boy scout stuff." In truth, the Canadian army was in no position to teach the men the real elements of soldiering. The army in Canada was not held in high esteem and the supply of trained instructors was deplorably low. Not until the regiment arrived in Britain did the men begin the serious training that would prepare them for war.

In the spring of 1940, following weeks of rumour, orders were received to move the Regiment to base training at Camp Borden near Barrie, Ontario.

In Jackson Park, on May 12, the Regiment bade an official farewell to the city of Windsor with an impressive Drumhead service, viewed by a large and enthusiastic crowd. An advance party under Capt. Knox left for Borden on May 23, followed two days later by the rest. With pipes playing and kilts swinging, the Essex Scottish paraded smartly through the city to the railway terminal, where it departed amid cheers and tears. For many whose faces pressed against the train windows it would be a final farewell.

Few of the men had ever been as uncomfortable as in those first days at Borden. Now the regiment lived under canvas. Rain greeted their arrival, and continued for two days as they pitched tents in the mud and tried to keep warm and dry. Then began intensive training. For a month they did close-order drill for 5 hours a day. More small-arms practice followed, including the handling of Borden's Lewis machine guns — those which still fired.

At Borden the men received their first medical inspection. It was, to say the least, cursory; a quick glance at eyes and ears, a few questions about family medical history, that was it. An old Scots veteran had told

Don, "Be careful when ye get intae the trenches. If a shell goes aff and ye cut yer upper lip, ye'll get lockjaw for sure." Don's response to this piece of medically suspect advice was to grow a mustache — a facial adornment which he retains to this day.

During the summer the other regiments training at Borden — those belonging to the 1st Division — left the camp for overseas. The men of the Essex Scottish knew their own departure was imminent. Don began to feel like a real soldier.

Finally they received word; a formal announcement by the colonel in the parade square, the acquisition of divisional shoulder flashes, final packing, last farewells, and on July 16 the regiment was packed into a troop train heading out toward the embarkation port.

CHAPTER TWO

The train trip to their embarkation point lasted two days. They didn't know where they were going, except that it was East. Boredom was relieved by continuous floating crap games and poker marathons. Meals were prepared at the railroad stations and handed to the troops at the brief stops the train made on its way to the East Coast. The military authorities, well aware of what several hundred healthy and confined soldiers could do to the Canadian National Railway's property, made sure there was no liquor on the train.

At Quebec City the train stopped for several hours and the men were given the opportunity to see the old walled city — in platoon formation, under the watchful eye of their officers. To the men from the deepest south-western Ontario, most of whom had never been further east than Toronto, the French-Canadian capital was a strange, foreign city with its narrow, winding cobblestone streets, its tin roofs and multitude of church spires, its steep lanes and stepped alleyways. The men from the flatlands of Windsor, Chatham and Wallaceburg felt that they had already reached a different country.

From Quebec City the train followed the shores of the St. Lawrence River into the Maritime Provinces. At Truro, Nova Scotia, Don and some of his friends found out from some women on the station platform that there was a bootlegger nearby willing to sell his stock. Within a few minutes, while the officers' attention was elsewhere, the Essex Scottish had cleaned him out.

Several hours later, wobbling on rubbery legs, they arrived in Halifax in the early evening of July 16th, and were immediately marched on to the Empress of Australia, a converted Canadian Pacific liner. Wartime regulations dictated a new name: she was now, rather ambitiously, E53. As the men marched up the gangways, they could see the liner's deck covered with gigantic packing cases — American aircraft and tanks destined for Britain?

In the summer of 1939 the regally refurbished Empress had transported King George VI and Queen Elizabeth across the Atlantic for an important pre-war tour of Canada. Twelve months later she had not been completely converted into a troopship and still retained many of the comforts of her peace time role; a full civilian complement of cigarettes and tobacco and , above deck, several reminders of her royal service could be found in the furniture, drapes and bathroom accessories. Don was below deck.

Although the men were gradually adopting to the hurry-up and wait mentality of army life, they became restless as hours turned to days and still they sat in Halifax harbour. The officers sensed the mounting tension and drained the bottled-up energy through a program of route marches in the city, and frequent life-boat drills. The soldier has little understanding of naval procedures, and the complexity of organizing a convoy to meet the rigours of the North Atlantic. The roving pack of German U-boats was playing a deadly game of cat and mouse with Allied shipping. To minimize the risks, hundreds of details had to be examined and analyzed before committing the convoy to sea. Finally at 1900 hours on July 23, 1940, the Empress, the last ship to leave its mooring, slipped out of the harbour and the process of convoy formation was underway.

As word spread that the Second Division was sailing Haligonians crowded the piers to say goodbye. In the deepening night pipes played as the ships left the security of the harbour — warm tears mixed with the salt spray on the faces of many men as the outline of Halifax receded into the darkness.

At sea most of the regiment dutifully lined up at the rails in a customary hommage that landlubbers pay to the heaving Atlantic. Don found himself quite unable to be seasick, even when topped up with lukewarm Watney, Bass, or Worthington's ale.

The trip took ten days and was quite uneventful. There was one explosion on the other side of the convoy, but, as far as the Empress of Australia was concerned, it might have been a peacetime crossing. Seasickness, constant life-boat drills, and endless poker games kept the men from damaging Canadian Pacific's maritime assets. The convoy was joined on July 30th by eight destroyers from Britain — a welcome sight to the Canadians, especially those who had lost all taste for the sea. They would soon be landing.

On August 1, the men lined the decks of the ship and watched the green hills of the Firth of Clyde slip by as they neared Gourock. For the majority of them it was the first glimpse of the British Isles. The bright summer sunshine was a welcome relief from the monotony of the grey North Atlantic. They anchored in the Firth and the ship's regimental pipe band treated the watchers to a noisy rendition of "Highland Laddie".

They disembarked in the late afternoon of day two, and boarded five trains for the journey to their new homes in the great army base of Aldershot. The men looked with curiosity at the narrow streets, the close-packed houses and tenements, and, strangest of all, the multitude of chimney pots on the roofs of the buildings. To men who had grown up in centrally-heated homes, it seemed that the British needed an awful lot of fires to keep warm. As the evening lengthened into night, and the train chugged south through towns and cities, they noticed another curious thing: no lights. The blackout was universal. As they passed through southern Scotland and into northern England, the carefree Canadians, just arrived from the bright lights of North America, became aware that the country through which they travelled, and which was to be their home for the foreseeable future, was a war zone.

By 5 p.m. the following evening they had disembarked from the trains and were marched in formation through Aldershot to Maida Barracks, preceded by the pipes and drums of the band.

After dumping their kit in their assigned platoon room, Don and Johnny Pidgeon from Windsor decided to seek out one of the famous British pubs that they had been talking about during the long journey south. After all, nobody had told them to stay in the barracks. They had been confined for the best part of two weeks, and it was high time they sampled the hospitality proffered in this most civilized of British institutions. One ale led to many, and the Canadians were most thoroughly and insouciantly blotto by the time they were ready to grope their way back through the unfamiliar, blacked-out streets to the base. As they arrived at the entrance to the barracks they heard a loud voice in the darkness:

"You two men! Come here and lend a hand."

"You go to hell!" they bawled back at the hidden inquirer. There was a brief pause, then the rapid shuffle of feet. Out of the gloom emerged the empurpled features of Captain Turnbull, the regimental adjutant, glaring at them with blood in his eye.

Fourteen days later they were released from confinement and rejoined their platoons. After a fortnight in the lockup, Don found even the sparse amenities of life in Maida Barracks a luxury. The men were housed by platoons, one to a large room in the massive brick and stone structures which made up the barracks. Each man slept on a folding metal bed with a straw tick and bolster, and kept his gear in a large wooden footlocker at the end of his bed. Heating was supplied by a single pot-bellied stove against one wall. Washing facilities, latrines and messhall were situated in a central block serving all the inhabitants of the barracks blocks. At one end of Maida Barracks was a NAAFI canteen, heavily frequented by Canadians eagerly seeking the company of female staff.

The very structure of Maida Barracks — its brick and stone Victorian solidity, with heavy wooden floors and massive doors, and the whole spit-and-polish atmosphere of the place penetrated the Canadians' consciousness. In southern Ontario, with the neutral United States visible across the border, everything in abundance and no blackout or air raids, they had been playing at war. Now, with the Battle of Britain being fought overhead, sharing in the life of a nation at war, living amongst professional soldiers who had already fought in France, the raw Canadians knew, deep down, that they still had a long way to go before they could really call themselves soldiers.

Under the eyes of the combat-experienced British they trained hard for the expected German invasion. They became proficient in the new weapons issued to the platoons; Bren guns, 2-inch mortars, anti-tank rifles. Headquarters Company was issued with Bren-gun carriers and the men were put through a rigorous routine of route marches, map exercises, and training in infantry-tank co-operation. Some nasty accidents took place before the infantrymen realized that it was their duty to keep out of the tanks' way, not vice-versa.

During their period in Aldershot they had their first taste of war, standing guard during air raids, and fighting fires started by German incendiaries. After they were declared fit to be classed as front-line troops, they were posted to defensive positions on the south coast. There they moved constantly between expected invasion points — Brighton, Hastings, Rye, Bognor Regis.

As the Battle of Britain petered out and the Germans switched to the night bombing campaign, it became clear that there would be no invasion that year. While there was no slow-down in defence preparations, the Canadians could afford to relax a little, and become familiar with the society they were helping to defend. Generally their relations with the civilians were extremely good — although they didn't always get along with the British soldiers. The regular British Army officers were inclined to view the new arrivals as undisciplined colonials who needed lessons in saluting and dress code. Until the first contingents of Americans arrived in 1942, the Canadians were often highly unpopular with the British soldiers for much the same reasons as the Americans were to become unpopular. The Canadians were lavishly paid by the standards of the British Army — at $1.30 a day, the Canadian private earned the equivalent of a British NCO. In addition the Canadians received large shipments of cigarettes from home which they would sell to the British troops on their pay day. The British soldiers were not averse to buying Sweet Caps, Winchesters or Buckinghams on the cheap, but it did place the Canadians in the role of rich cousins lording it over their poor relatives. There were many brawls in pubs where the British soldiers were enraged by the free-spending Canadians who monopolized what they considered to be their beer and their girls.

There were other ways in which the Canadians antagonized their British counterparts. The Canadians could generally afford to have their uniforms altered, the rough material could be finely shaved until it looked like an officer's uniform freshly acquired from Gieves of London. With razor-sharp creases, ties (ready to be hidden under battledress collars at the approach of an officer), glittering brass buttons and swagger sticks under their arms, the dress of the Essex Scottish in particular out classed the shapeless khakis of the average Tommy. The Canadians were mightily relieved when the Americans arrived to replace them as objects of envy.

There were a few diversions for the men. Many of them had relatives in Britain, and issuing of passes for weekend leaves saw an exodus of Essex Scottish to towns and villages from Inverness to Penzance, laden with cartons of cigarettes and tins of butter for long-lost cousins, uncles and grand-parents. As in all wars, romance bloomed between soldiers and local girls, and marriages were promised to girls all over England. Some of those promises were honoured. The NAAFI and the garrison theatre were heavily patronized: at the latter, the Canadians were at last able to see in the flesh the artists they had heard on the CBC before the war, like Gracie Fields, Tessie O'Shea, and Vera Lynn.

The main off-duty occupation, as for troops of every nationality in Britain, was visiting the pubs. With beer at sixpence a pint, the Canadians could afford to out-drink their British counterparts, to the occasional detriment of Anglo-Canadian relations. Regiments had their own favorite pubs, and many became territorial about them. The Essex Scottish were not particularly welcome at the places patronized by the Royal Hamilton Light Infantry, and the Royal Canadian Regiment did not welcome intruders from the Seaforth Highlanders of Canada, and so on. British soldiers stayed away from pubs known to be the haunts of Canadians, and French-Canadian troops stayed away from the pubs known to be the preserves of their English-speaking fellow-countrymen. It was a kind of natural division of territory, and nobody thought there was anything sinister in it.

The pubs were the bane of Don's service career. Every time he won a promotion to lance-corporal, the old army custom of "wetting the stripes" had to be observed, and the free-spending Canadians usually overstepped the bounds of propriety, military discipline and barracks bedtime, with the consequence that the stripes stayed on his arm only on a temporary basis — at least while there was no prospect of action. On one occasion, after a promotion to lance-corporal, he was observed by a police constable to be making a slow and unsteady progress down a street in the middle of the blackout, solemnly inspecting the numbers on each civilian doorway, and mumbling something about, "Whish onsh Maida Barracksh." The constable observed him tiring of the search and curling up in the last doorway on the street to take a nap, and called for reinforcements.

Don's next memory was of waking with a raging thirst in a cell in the local police station. The door clanked open.

"Here y'are, Canada, this'll set you right." A large, friendly policeman stood above him, holding an immense mug of steaming tea. Surprised at the treatment, Don drank it down while he waited for Sergeant Adams of the Essex Scottish to pick him up and take him back to the barracks.

He spent the next fourteen days in the familiar surroundings of the lockup to contemplate his sins, a contemplation broken at frequent intervals by the cleaning of barrack rooms, latrines and corridors, and the scrubbing of pots and pans.

And there were visitors, from newsreel crews recording regimental activities for the movie theatres of Windsor and Wallaceburg, to VIPs. Most of the latter were welcomed — like King George VI, Anthony Eden, and Lord Louis Mountbatten. One, however, was booed loudly by the Essex Scottish, among others, when he appeared at Aldershot. This was the Canadian Prime Minister Mackenzie King. In part it was the miserable weather on the day of his appearance, in part it was the Canadian forces' lack of employment in a war zone, but it was also due to the growing dislike of a Prime Minister who refused to impose conscription in a war where most other countries were even conscripting women. Whatever the reason, the Canadian Prime Minister received the royal raspberry from his loyal troops when he made a speech to them on August 23, 1941.

The lack of engagement for the Canadian Second Division in a war zone did have its compensations. With a couple of five pound notes tucked in a breast pocket, and a kit-bag tightly packed with tinned meat, butter, nylons and cartons of cigarettes, the enlisted men could tour the Isles in style. As a teenager, Don's father had emigrated to Canada from Bexhill-on-Sea. Don took advantage of week-end passes to visit relatives. Family gatherings were festive affairs and Don, with his gift for exaggerated tales of life in the colonies, was often the centre of attention. As pleasant as these gatherings were, and deep as Don's cultural roots were in the rich soil of Sussex, it was Scotland that caught his imagination.

Scottish influence was strong in his home town of Wallaceburg named for the Scottish patriot William Wallace. The area had been settled by Highlanders from the Western Isles brought to Baldoon by Lord Selkirk in 1804. In school Don's interest was further kindled by reading the historical accounts of the early Scottish explorers — Fraser, Thompson, and MacKenzie. Whatever the influences, Scotland had struck a chord in him. Don made detailed plans to spend his first extended leave touring the Highlands.

He did not travel beyond Edinburgh. In the evening of a bitterly cold February day in 1941, Don arrived at Waverley station with a freshly-inked ten-day pass in his wallet. He checked into the Victoria League Club on Princes Street intending to head northward the following day. A hotel porter told him of a dance for servicemen at the Palais in Fountainbridge. It was all the encouragement Don needed. Off he went, hoping to meet a Scottish lass who might welcome the advances of a diminutive red-haired Canadian.

The dance hall was intimate with a dimly-lighted horseshoe balcony providing a haven for adventurous young lovers. The featured attraction, a professional dance band, played romantic ballads. A bitterly cold wind howled outside and the rhythmic swaying of the dancers inside created a romantic mood unequalled by Hollywood.

The mood was inescapable. Don had noticed a particularly attractive young woman with auburn hair. She was undoubtedly an excellent dancer for she rarely sat out a number. When he asked her to dance she graciously accepted. As one dance succeeded the last, Don felt himself attracted to this woman, a feeling he had not often experienced before. But his request to escort her home was refused. Not wishing to be impolite to the engaging young Canadian, she suggested he call upon her and

Don and Helen Neill in the autumn of 1941.

her widowed mother the following day for tea. This ploy had gently dampened the ardour of many previous suitors, but Don was not deterred.

The following afternoon, all thoughts of the Highlands forgotten, Don appeared at the doorway of 124 Gorgie Rd. A surprised and flustered Helen Neill greeted him. Following a hurried introduction to her mother, Helen escaped to the kitchen to prepare the tea. By the time she returned with the tray her mother had uncapped a highly prized bottle of Scotch whisky. It was the least she could do for a brave young laddie from Canada prepared to sacrifice his life in defence of Britain. By leave's end Don had completely captivated the mother, but Helen was less enthusiastic. Among her friends too many war-time romances had ended tragically. She did not wish to suffer the same fate.

Whatever Helen's thoughts might be, Don refused to be forgotten. During the following year, he spent every available leave in Edinburgh. Moon-light strolls along the Royal Mile, window-shopping on Princes Street, picnics in the park, and late evening dining in hospitable pubs eventually weakened Helen's resolve. Soon they had their favorite pubs, the Clock, or sometimes the Waterloo, where they met when Helen finished work. Sundays they travelled by tram to the Wheat Sheaf on the outskirts of Edinburgh. In the land of John Knox alcoholic beverages were not sold on the Sabbath except to weary travellers. A thirty minute ride on an Edinburgh tram certainly qualified for this special privilege.

In February 1942, almost a year to the day since he first met Helen, Don proposed marriage. They were in an alcove of the Waterloo pub enjoying a fine wine. Helen still had her doubts about war-time romances, but she was now deeply in love with her spirited Canadian and accepted. They pocketed their wine glasses, courtesy of the management. That weekend they carried out a tradition of the Wheat Sheaf by hurling their wine glasses into the fireplace, thus assuring the good fortune of the final toast — and giving the lie to the gross calumny of Scottish thrift.

Helen and Don made plans for a late September wedding, 1942. But the Canadian government and the War Office were also making plans — plans that would end all hope for a fall wedding, and would bring about the trials of war-time romance that Helen had tried to avoid. Dieppe, a small resort town on the channel coast of France, was selected as the site of the Allies' first division-strength raid on Occupied Europe. This was scheduled for the summer of 1942.

But the regiments of Canada's Second Division were unaware of the extent to which their destinies were being shaped by their political and military leaders. They knew only that they were tired of waiting, and that the waiting and false alarms were having an effect on the regiments. Other Commonwealth troops were fighting, in North Africa and the Far East, and the Royal Canadian Air Force had been in the thick of the air fighting since the campaign in France. The Navy too had been fighting even before Canada's formal declaration of war on September 10th, 1939, but the army had been doing little except to guard the south coast of England. They wanted action, and their government was unwilling to send troops to fight with other Commonwealth forces in the war zones.

So for the Second Canadian Division it was a case of simulated war; more route marches, manoeuvres, simulated air attacks, gas drills, fire watches, more route marches, training with the tanks, map drills, more route marches. It was after one of these manoeuvres that Don wearily dragged himself back into barracks and saw a familiar figure sitting at the foot of his bed.

"Hi, Don," he said.

Don stared at him. "Vic! I thought. . . . ." then he noticed the new regimental flash on his shoulder: Essex Scottish.

"But you're supposed to be in the RCRs."

"Thought I'd come and look after my little brother. Where's the canteen?"

Vic was, in a sense, a replacement. Angus, all six feet and four inches of him, had become a military policeman in the Provost Corps, where even the rowdy Canadians were intimidated by his size. So Vic had come to look after his brother. Oddly, he seemed to spend just as much time in the guardhouse as his kid brother had.

Things were looking up. On January 27, 1942, the Essex Scottish received a new commander. Lieutenant-Colonel Jasperson was a tough soldier, and under his leadership the regiment's professionalism was enhanced. The pace of the exercises and manoeuvres picked up. Something was in the wind, but no one knew what. Meanwhile, they kept watch over the south coast and drank the pubs dry from Sussex to Hampshire.

After more than eighteen months of shuttling between defensive points along the south coast, and with no immediate prospects of action, Don began to chafe at the routine. It seemed that of all the Commonwealth and Empire armies in the war only the Canadians were sitting it out. British, Australian, New Zealand, South African, and Indian troops were heavily engaged in the Middle East as the Eighth Army engaged in see-saw battles with the Afrika Korps. British Commandos were involved in hit-and-run engagements along enemy-occupied coasts, and when Don got word of the formation of a Canadian Commando "Viking Force" he immediately volunteered. It was against the infantryman's first instincts, as well as his principles, to volunteer for anything, but Commando training was a whole lot more interesting than sitting on his hands in Bognor Regis.

CHAPTER THREE

The Viking Force was as motley a group as ever graced the Canadian Army. As its commander, Major Brian McCool, soon found out, it was a collection of the best and the worst in the Canadian Second Division. Each of the nine regiments in the Division sent a dozen men and an officer when the call went out for volunteers. Some sent their most skilled and intelligent men, others regarded the Vikings as a convenient dumping-ground for their trouble makers. The latter were quickly weeded out by the demanding McCool: those who remained were men of initiative and enterprise, soldiers who were tired of army training routine and wanted to be challenged.

The Vikings were formed in imitation of the British Commandos

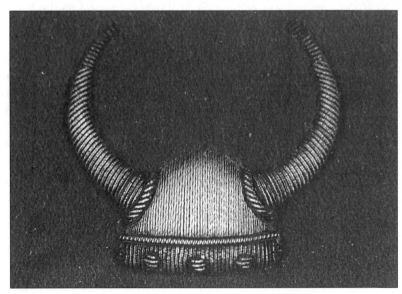

The Viking insignia – never worn.

*Major Brian McCool (left)
on board the
Josephine Charlotte
with the ship's Captain.*

who were then carrying out lightning raids on the coasts of occupied Europe. Major McCool, a disciplinarian from the Royal Regiment of Canada, trained his men hard, teaching more refined military skills to soldiers already well-versed, but untested in the rougher aspects of infantry combat. Their initial training took place at Seaford, by the Seven Sisters cliffs on the Sussex coast, an area of rough and rugged terrain by English standards. There the men could practice cliff assaults, concealment, and field-craft, in preparation for the more exacting training that awaited them later in Scotland.

Don found himself with two buddies from Aldershot, Mac Moloy and Clinton Judd. Don and Clint were billeted in stables attached to a disused summer camp. Though the stables were comfortable, the food was inadequate for men engaged in strenuous daily exercise, so they became experts at snaring the rabbits which infested the area. Every evening after supper the stables were filled with the aroma of rabbit frying in butter over the old wood stove which heated the draughty building. Hardship could be enjoyable, given enough snare wire and a loose window in the unit kitchen building.

Compared to the square-bashing atmosphere of Aldershot, the life of a trainee Commando at Seaford was almost idyllic. There was no set time for Lights Out. The men could spend all night on the town if they wanted, as long as they were able to complete a fifteen mile route march, or spend a day climbing cliffs, if that was what McCool ordered for the day. Their commander himself set the example: on most mornings he could be seen jogging in his shorts before breakfast.

The routine varied considerably. One day it would be training in unarmed combat, another day they would practice with the unit weapons — Brens and 2-inch mortars, as well as with their personal weapons — rifles, tommy guns and grenades. They learned how to kill silently with a strangling wire or a Commando knife, how to find their way in the dark, and how to use their escape kits, which contained maps, French money, and concentrated bars of chocolate which could last for days as an invader's diet. At other times, they learned how to deal with tanks by leaping on top and dropping a grenade down the hatch — almost the only way for them, since they would not be carrying anti-tank weapons on operations.

Some of the training was downright unpleasant. As commandos, they were expected to strike silently and efficiently from the sea. In preparation, they went out in fishing boats in the roughest weather to test their susceptibility to sea-sickness. Most could cope, but others were incapacitated by the pitching and rolling of the little Sussex fishing boats, to the derision of the civilian crews, who made their daily living in the temperamental waters of the Channel. Some of Canada's finest became so sick in the uncontrollable motion that they would have thrown themselves overboard if they had the strength to do so. All of them, however, were thrown over the side as part of their training — with full packs. They had to show their ability to survive in all conditions, even if the Army killed them in the process.

Gradually their numbers were whittled down. They were given a chance to show what they could do. Those who measured up to McCool's stringent standards stayed; the others returned to their units. Those who had volunteered for the challenge found themselves in a unit where the normal army regulations did not apply. They were treated as men, and responded accordingly. As long as they brought a disciplined, professional attitude to their work, what they did in their off-duty hours was of no concern to the Army. Leisure time, when it wasn't spent killing and eating the rabbit population of Sussex, consisted mainly of visiting the pubs of Newhaven and Seaford.

The entertainment available was the usual soldier's escape from hard routine; drinking and brawling. On one occasion several of the Vikings, with some of the British Commandos in tow, managed to accomplish the slapstick feat of ramming someone through the base drum belonging to the band in the dance hall they were patronizing. It was unfortunate that the individual jammed in the drum happened to belong to the Irish Guards, and was accompanied by, it seemed, half his regiment. The resulting donnybrook established that commando training could enable even a handful of British and Canadian commandos to emerge victorious over the pride of the Guards. The next morning the news of the victory was all over the camp. McCool just smiled and kept his own counsel.

As individuals, the Vikings could also take good care of themselves. On one black midnight as Don was making his unsteady way along the top of the cliffs to the camp he was assaulted by several civilians who had been hiding in the gorse. Even with the lack of co-ordination engendered by several pints of best Bass, his Commando training emerged in a series of violent reflexes which put a quick end to the attack. Grinning in smug satisfaction at his military professionalism, the diminutive Viking tottered wearily into the stable, flopped on his bunk and passed out. Next morning, as he was explaining the bruises to Judd, he noticed his Fairbairn dagger was missing. Feeling suddenly unwell, he tried to remember just how he had beaten off his attackers above the cliffs.

"Only one thing for it," said Judd. "Let's go back to where they jumped you."

Accompanied by Judd and several gleefully anticipating Vikings, Don walked back along the cliffs, searching for bodies. There were none to be found. Suddenly there was a shout behind him and his bowels turned to jelly. He looked round to see Judd bending over beside a posted notice board, "What's he looking at," thought Don as he ran back.

Actually Judd wasn't looking at anything. He was doubled over with laughter, tears streaming down his cheeks as he pointed shakily at the board. In bold letters it said DANGER, CLIFFS. Rammed through the centre was Don's dagger!

A few weeks later they broke camp and embarked on the assault ship Josephine Charlotte for further training in Scotland. Their new home was the ship, permanently moored in Loch-na-Kiel off the Isle of Mull. Here, amid the rugged coves and wild hills of the island, the Vikings trained with the British Commandos, using live ammunition to reinforce the notion that it was not a bad idea to keep one's head down when the bullets were flying. The Vikings' days were filled with early-morning runs and route marches. Major McCool had them covering ten miles an hour with weapons and 60 pound packs, jumping from cliffs into sand pits fifteen feet below, climbing hundreds of feet up rock faces and making difficult river crossings. In the two latter activities, which were supposed to be taught by the British Commandos, the Canadians had already become so proficient and innovative that they ended up teaching their methods to their erstwhile mentors.

As the smallest of the group, at 5' 5" and 110 pounds, Don became the indispensable first man over the top, as the huskier Vikings found they could throw him about like a bale of hay on cliff-scaling exercises. On one occasion, his indispensability nearly came to an end when he fell out of his boat into the water. Loaded down with grenades, he was rescued by two quick-witted Vikings who grabbed him just before he sank to the bottom of the Atlantic.

Imperceptibly, Commando training for the Vikings became all work and very little play. From their floating home the Vikings made assault landings on the shores of Mull, and engaged in mock battles with the British Commando units training in the same area. If they didn't get back to the beaches after night manoeuvres in time to catch the landing craft back to the Charlotte, they faced an icy swim to the ship — and they couldn't leave their equipment on shore either. It was the best possible incentive to do their job properly and quickly. In these engagements, initiative and small-group tactics were stressed, rather than the platoon and section-level tactics of the regular army units. The men could approach objectives silently, they could kill sentries in a hundred different ways, and they could demolish almost any object, man-made or natural, which stood in their way. In all of this there was an almost complete absence of the usual discipline, and no great insistence that the men conform to the dress regulations of the Canadian Army. Performance, not spit and polish, were what McCool wanted from his men, and he got it.

McCool also made sure that his men got a regular ration of Navy rum, which was a good thing since the Vikings had drunk the pubs of Bunessan, the only town nearby, dry within a few days of their arrival. It was a long time between supply ferries to the island.

By the end of their training the Canadian Vikings were among the most highly trained troops in the British Isles. They had become the most thoroughly professional force in the Second Division, and the rumours flew round the force as to where their talents would be employed. Some swore that they were about to receive an issue of light-weight uniforms for North Africa; others had heard that they were going to receive winter outfits for an invasion of Norway.

These rumours turned out to be false. As ordained by the higher powers in Ottawa, and at the British War Office, rumour was the closest the Vikings ever came to an operation as a unit. In the early summer of 1942 this highly-trained and eager striking force was broken up. Every private became a lance-corporal, and returned to his regiment bearing the insignia of Combined Operations on his shoulder. The higher powers had something in mind for them. But none of the Second Division's Vikings had the faintest idea what it was.

CHAPTER FOUR

Where was the Second Division headed? The men had no idea. Don and the rest of the ex-Vikings, with new stripes on their arms, and bearing the wings, anchor, and tommy-gun insignia of Combined Ops, knew only that they were being trained to exhaustion in hit-and-run warfare. The Vikings taught the division the refinements of cliff-climbing, assault landings, hand-to-hand combat, the silent killing of sentries, demolitions — the whole array of destructive skills taught them on the Isle of Mull. The men of the division wanted action. While the British Army was engaged in the Western Desert and in the Far East, the Canadians were guarding British homes and escorting British women. Sussex, Kent, Hampshire, and Dorset soldiers were being killed and wounded in the war while the Canadians had not set foot on a battlefield since the First Divisions' foray in France in the summer of 1940. Other Commonwealth troops — Australians, New Zealanders, South Africans — were part of the Eighth Army in North Africa. The Canadians felt their position with acute discomfort. They wanted to prove something to the British as well as to themselves.

Since April 1942 Lord Mountbatten had a contribution in mind for the Canadians. Encouraged by the successful Commando raid on St. Nazaire the previous month, he set to work planning a more ambitious raid on Dieppe. The plan was indeed ambitious. There had been no large-scale amphibious assault on a fortified area since the attack on the Zeebrugge submarine base on April 23, 1918. British forces had conducted small-scale lightning raids on the coasts of Norway and France since early 1940, but the idea of assaulting a coastal town and holding it, even for a few hours, had hitherto been considered beyond the resources of the British forces.

The British had already learned the lessons of conducting land and sea operations without adequate air cover off Norway, Greece, Crete, and Malaya. The long tale of sunken ships and retreating armies had driven home a hard lesson. Dieppe was within reasonable range for fighter cover from the RAF, but the topography of the target area presented serious problems. The original plan of flank assaults on either side of the town, designed to converge and "pinch out" the area was discarded. The only reasonably level beach area was in front of Dieppe itself. The rest of the coast was largely cliffs rising sheer from the high-water line.

The plan for the Dieppe raid — Operation Rutter — called for the main assault to be supported by tanks landed on the main beaches, with two flank attacks at Pourville and Puys. The whole operation was to be preceded by a heavy aerial bombardment to destroy the Germans' system of beach defences. By the beginning of May it was decided that the Canadian Second Division should constitute the main assault force. The First Canadian Corps Headquarters issued "Training Instruction No. 9" to the First, Second and Third Divisions, providing for combined operations training for all three divisions. This was to cover the fact that only one of them was to carry out the landing. It was this training period that saw the Vikings running their Second Division comrades ragged over the beaches, cliffs and fields of the Isle of Wight.

On June 11th and 12th the division rehearsed for the raid with a mock-assault on the seaside town of Bridport, Dorset. The rehearsal was a disaster. Assault craft landed troops miles away from their designated areas, and the Tank Landing Craft were an hour late in reaching the beaches. Even when the men got over the beaches, their progress inland was extremely slow. Against even the lightest of German opposition it was clear that the landings would have been a catastrophe. This test, exercise "Yukon", was followed by "Yukon II" which was more successful, although the craft carrying the Essex Scottish managed to land their troops late after losing their way on the run in to the beach.

However, Mountbatten was satisfied, and he decided that "Rutter" should go ahead at the earliest opportunity.

On July 2 Don lined up his men, and, with the rest of the Essex Scottish, climbed into the trucks that were ostensibly to take them on another exercise. Instead, they were taken aboard the assault landing ships and told that instead of exercise "Klondike", they were to become a part of the first division-strength raid on Occupied France. Lord Mountbatten and the Second Division commander, General Roberts, visited the men, now sealed off from contact with the rest of the world, and told them about their duties in the coming raid. The elation and nervousness among the troops was palpable. Action at last! A chance to show that the Canadian Army of 1942 was the equal of the Canadian Army of the First World War. The men waited for the throb of the turbines which would tell them they were on the way to fight the enemy. All around the Isle of Wight, the ships of the assault force and their escort gathered and prepared to set off. In the big landing ships, the men of the Second Division sat and waited, writing letters, cleaning weapons, filling ammunition pouches. In addition to the Essex Scottish, there were the men of the Hamilton Light Infantry, the Royal Regiment of Canada, the Queen's Own Cameron Highlanders of Canada, the South Saskatchewan Regiment, Les Fusiliers Mont-Royale, and the men of the Calgary Regiment with their Churchill tanks.

But the weather grew more unsettled, and the commanders kept putting off the raid. It was scheduled for July 4, but the day came and went and still the weather refused to co-operate. A few more days and the tides would be unsuitable for a landing at Dieppe. The days dragged on and the men became more and more fretful over the delays. Then, on July 7, the ships at anchor were the target of a German air raid. It was a small one — four Focke-Wulf-fighter bombers — but the Princess Astrid and the Princess Josephine Charlotte were slightly damaged. More importantly, the Germans could hardly fail to suspect that something was afoot, with some 200 vessels in the area. Still, there was one more suitable day on which to mount the raid. But on July 8 it was cancelled. Aboard the Prince Charles, Don cursed along with the rest of the regiment. After so much training, and the tension of the past few days, to be ready for action and now this! They disembarked and were taken by truck back to barracks. They got thoroughly drunk, to hide their disappointment as much as to relieve the tension. The raid was off — so they thought.

The raid was off — but only for a month. The men were back in camps and barracks, going through the dreary routines of soldiers far from the front. The assault ships had been unloaded and were back at their usual duty of participating in troop exercises. The Armada of escort vessels slated to support the "Rutter" operation was dispersed to fight the Germans elsewhere. Security had broken down, and everybody on the South Coast knew that a raid on Dieppe had been cancelled.

But political decisions and military plans combined to give the Second Division another chance. Once more the roads to Newhaven, Gosport, Shoreham, Portsmouth and Southhampton were filled with trucks as Canadian soldiers and British Commandos moved to the embarkation points. Once more Don got his squad together and embarked with the Essex Scottish on the Prince Charles at Portsmouth. Many thought this was just another exercise until Mountbatten himself came aboard and gave them a pep talk on what they were going to do to the Germans once they landed in France.

In the late afternoon of August 18 the minesweepers left Portsmouth to sweep clear channels ahead of the ships and escorts of the raiding force. It was one of the most beautiful evenings of an unpredictable summer, warm, with the sea a glassy calm. At 5 p.m. the Prince Charles moved slowly from its berth to join the fleet gathering for the journey to France. For the men of the regiment the fleet steaming so purposefully to the enemy coast was the largest gathering of ships they had ever seen. Everywhere in the gathering gloom, slipping through the placid waters toward the enemy coast, there were the grey warships of the Royal Navy, bristling with guns ready to blast a path ashore for the infantry-men in the assault force. To the men in the boats, knowing little of the capabilities of the different categories of naval vessels, it was an impres-sive display. The fact that there was no warship in the fleet larger than a destroyer, no gun larger that a 4.7″ dual-purpose, was something that held little meaning for the troops. The Royal Navy, having suffered dis-astrous losses in heavy ships at the hands of the Luftwaffe, the U-boats and the Japanese Navy and Air Force in the past year, could no longer risk cruisers or battleships in coastal waters. From the outset, the Dieppe raid was deprived of the blasting power of the Navy's huge floating artillery. It was not a mistake that Combined Operations would make again after Dieppe, but the Second Division, nearing the French coast, in the deceptively peaceful dawn of August 18, was not to know that. For most of the raiding force twelve hours later it didn't matter anyway.

One other aspect of the raid's planning should have worried them had they known about it The heavy bomber attack, which had been timed to take place just before the raid began, had been called off. Now, only fighter-bombers were to strike at defensive positions of the target before the landing craft grounded. In effect, the defenders at Dieppe were to get off lightly. The attacking troops had to rely on surprise, and speed in getting over the beaches and into the town, rather than a crush-ing weight of ordnance on the defenders.

In the grey dark of the channel the assault boats were lowered, and the troops clambered down the sides of the Prince Charles using ropes, and took their places in the bumpy, flat- bottomed craft that would run

them up on the enemy beaches. Everywhere in the faint light before
dawn khaki-clad troops were doing the same thing, following the strict
timetables of the Admiralty and the army brass who had designed the
operation. The men settling down in the bobbing shoeboxes, designed
to land them on hostile shores, were the leading edge of a military enterprise planned for months, and approved by the highest authorities in
Britain and Canada. The operation was a matter of high strategic planning, a part of the overall grand design to bring Germany to her knees.
To the men, bounced around in their little boats on the way to France,
the gods of the War Office and the cabinet rooms were unthought of .
The Essex Scottish were going into action. That — and the fact that
many of the regiment were seasick — was of more immediate impor-
tance.

As they chugged through the water, under a thin ribbon of grey light
in the eastern sky, Don looked at his men. All of them were quiet, grip-
ping their weapons as they crouched below gunwale level to escape the
flying spray. For the first time, corporal Errey began to worry about his
section, about his responsibilities to his men. They were all going into
battle for the first time, the training over and the game afoot. He
clutched his Thompson sub-machine gun tighter as he waited for the
sudden roar of naval gunfire, and the grinding of gravel beneath their
hull, which would announce their landing on the beaches of France.

CHAPTER FIVE

Their landing area was designated "Red Beach", directly in front of the town. Their objective was to take the eastern end of the town, which included the harbour and the hotels along the sea front. The Hamilton Light Infantry, on their right flank, was to capture the buildings along the western end of the sea front, including the big casino that was Dieppe's biggest peace-time attraction. Behind the two infantry battalions were the LCTs (Landing Craft Tank) carrying the Calgary Tank Regiment, and the floating reserve of Les Fusiliers Mont-Royale. The plan was straightforward and should have presented few difficulties for well-supported troops. Once they were over the sea wall and into the town itself, supported by the tanks and sappers and engineers, the Essex Scottish and the RHLI (Royal Hamilton Light Infantry) would have a tough time of it, but they knew they could carry out the job they had come to do.

No one knew, as the boats neared the beaches in the brightening dawn, that the necessary fire support was not there. In military terms the impressive display of naval ordnance booming behind them in the distance was little more than fireworks: the heavy cruisers and battleships necessary to lay down drenching fire on the defenders could not be spared by a navy reeling from terrible losses in the Mediterranean and the Far East. The flights of Hurricanes roaring overhead to strafe the German positions along the front of Dieppe were well-timed, but of little use in silencing fortified machine-gun and mortar posts. The RAF's heavy bombers were not spared to demolish the positions which the navy couldn't destroy. The morning, which opened with the bright promise of surprise, quickly became a nightmare of slaughter to which the Canadians could make little effective reply. Few of them ever made their way inland, and fewer got back to the beaches. Dieppe's beaches became a deathtrap — a killing ground where the soldiers of the

Canadian Second Division were easy targets for the German troops.

The men were silent as the boat neared the shore. Clutching his Thompson, Don tensed near the bow of the craft as the engine's note changed on the final run-in. Over to his right, came the booming sound of an enemy shore battery. The ramp went down with a rattle of chains and a splash from the bow as the boat shuddered to a halt. Don raced out with the rest and splashed into the shallow water. Everywhere along Red and White Beaches, the Canadians hit the enemy-held shores with perfect timing, in regular formation. For a few seconds, as the men raced in a khaki tide up the shores to the sea wall, it looked as if the Germans had been caught unprepared.

With a shattering suddenness, Don found himself walking into a wall of noise. The Germans opened up with all available weapons as the Canadian infantry raced up the open beaches. Streams of machine-gun fire laced across the shingle and spattered on the bows of the landing craft, kicking up little fountains of water, spraying fragments of shingle everywhere, finding targets in the boats and on the pebbly beach. As the infantry tried to win the race for the sea wall, men fell all over the beaches, dropping like marionettes whose strings have been cut . Between the landing craft and the sea wall lay two tangled rows of barbed wire. The troops crossed them using the methods they had been taught in battle training — some men dropped on the wire, while others leaped over, using their comrades as stepping stones. With the pack on his back, cradling the tommy-gun in his arms, Don tried to outrace the streams of machine-gun bullets which all sounded as if they had his number. One stretch of wire . . . somebody falls on it . . . leap over . . . on to the next — somebody on it — jump . . . more fire, bullets rattling and pinging off the hard shingle. With his breath knifing into his lungs, Don threw himself into a depression near the base of the sea wall and gasped like a stranded fish, safe at last from the malevolent crossfire of concealed — and undamaged — German pillboxes along the beach and in the headlands.

He looked back. Along the whole length of the beaches the shingle was covered with men who looked like bundles of khaki rags, some of them moving slowly, most of them lying still. More men poured over the barbed wire to the sea wall. Some of them reached it. Others fell, on the shingle, on the wire — many of them never even made it out of the boats. In a few seconds Red Beach had turned into a slaughterhouse. At the shoreline the boats of the first wave, many of them loaded with dead and wounded who had never stepped on French soil, backed off and tried to make room for the LCTs carrying the Calgary Tanks. The men pinned under the precarious shelter of the sea wall and crouched in the depressions on the beach, not daring to raise their heads, needed help.

The din increased, as the shore batteries sent fountains of water towering over the melee of retreating and incoming boats. The German mortar batteries opened up and sprayed the men on the beach with high explosive, shrapnel and more of the vicious fragments of shingle, which were proving to be as deadly as machine-gun bullets.

It was quickly clear to Don that there was no way of getting off the beach and into the town. From behind the sea wall, the Germans began pitching grenades among the men. The Canadian Officers' attempts to organize assaults over the wall and into the town were defeated almost before they started. Several attempts were made and the men shot down as soon as they attempted to get over the wall. With no chance to get close to the enemy, Don's tommy-gun was useless. He threw it away and picked up a rifle from a dead soldier, looking for some visible target to fire at.

It was the same desperate story up and down Red and White Beaches. The Royal Hamilton Light Infantry and the Essex Scottish were being decimated by the concealed machine-guns and the invisible mortar and artillery positions of the Germans. The Germans were obviously not short of ammunition — the continuous roar of exploding shells, and the unceasing rattle and whine of machine-gun bursts, made it difficult to think even about personal safety. Men tried to get over the sea wall, or ran to what they thought were places of concealment, but were shot down before they had taken more than a few steps.

Where were the Calgary tanks? The arrival of the seaborne armour was their only hope of getting off the beaches and into the town. At the rate the infantry was being killed, the tanks would make little difference if they didn't show up soon. The men crouched in their scanty cover, and waited for them to arrive.

They had no contact with the other beaches. They couldn't know about the disaster awaiting the Royal Regiment at Puys, or the partial success of the Camerons and South Sasks at Pourville. On the flanks, the Commandos had achieved their objectives. But these were the only victories on that catastrophic morning. The main force was in the midst of a first-class military fiasco.

In the boiling inferno of Red Beach, Don shifted from one hole to another, somehow remaining untouched by the mortar bursts and the streams of machine-gun fire. There were no officers capable of giving him orders, and all he received for his efforts was an arsefull of shingle fragments spattered at him by a mortar burst. Nursing his tender injury he lay on his stomach in a shell hole and watched as naval ordnance rained down on German positions too well camouflaged and too strongly-built to suffer much from the destroyers' popguns.

A second wave arrived on the beaches. From his shelter in a shallow depression in the shingle, Don watched as the Canadian Engineers jumped from the craft dragging heavy loads of chespaling — rolls of snowfence — to help the following Calgary tanks get up the beaches. They were massacred trying to get the fence into position across the shingle on the exposed beaches. There was no hope: it was like shooting ducks in a pond.

The tanks arrived in their lumbering LCTs. Don watched as one LCT hit a sandbar and dropped its ramp. In a fatally premature move, the tank moved off the ramp and disappeared in the deep water beyond the sandbar. More LCTs rambled up to the beaches and disgorged their cargoes. The heavy Churchill tanks, in action for the first time, lumbered up the shingle. Without the chespaling to help them across the loose pebbles, most of them grounded in the shifting surface. The noise on the beaches rose to a deafening crescendo, worse than anything yet as the Germans threw everything in their armory at the tanks. Shore batteries, mortars, anti-tank guns and machine-guns zeroed in on the tanks. None of the German missiles penetrated the thick armour of the Churchills, but for the men on the beaches the casualties mounted. The tanks were immobile in the shingle, but their six-pounders could reply in kind to any German positions they could find in the chaos of the beaches.

Snipers and machine-gunners made the signallers their special target. Units lost contact with each other and with the ships out in the Channel. Don kept shifting along the beach in front of the Casino, looking for orders. In the confusion of that morning the only orders he was receiving were to the effect that if he didn't keep his bloody head down he wouldn't keep it very long.

The horrible events of the long, long day ran through his mind. First, the charge up the beach to the sea wall — that was bad enough. Then the arrival of the tanks on the beaches, which shifted most of the German fire to their immediate area. Finally, with most tanks out of action, the rain of fire increased once more as the shore batteries sent fountains of water towering over additional landing craft approaching the beach. The Fusiliers Mont-Royale were coming in to support them

— although what they could do except get themselves killed was impossible to imagine. The flimsy craft grounded, the ramps went down, and the Fusiliers valiantly charged up the beach. Those on the beach shouted to go back — but it was too late. Those who survived to the sea wall got under whatever cover they could and tried to stay alive.

The RAF sent in a force of fighter-bombers to relieve the pressure on the fire-swept beaches. The Hurricanes peeled off one by one and swept the area with cannon fire. Inevitably some of the shells spattered along the beaches, causing casualties among the raiding force. Finally, mercifully, the word came that they were to evacuate the beaches.

At last! Well, the Germans could have a souvenir. Don pulled the pins on a couple of grenades and put them in a shallow hole in the ground. He laid a pistol on the grenades to hold the levers down, and spread some shingle over them. Any enemy soldier wanting a souvenir of the day's sport was welcome to pick up the Webley and stand on the spot admiring it. Don intended to be safely in a pub in Newhaven by that time.

Once more, the RAF came in low over the beaches, this time to lay a smokescreen over the retreating soldiers. The order came through: "Everybody who can walk — four men take one wounded and run like hell to the boats!" Don and three others picked up a badly-wounded soldier by the arms and legs and ran through the smoke and the unrelenting German fire to the incoming landing craft. The Germans shifted their fire to the vulnerable boats as they crept in to the beaches. Don and his party reached the water and started to splash towards the nearest boat. The man they were carrying was dead by the time they reached the water. They dropped the body and splashed frantically towards the boat. Fountains of water rose in the air and machine-gun fire rattled and ricocheted off the steep steel sides of the LCTs as they neared the shoreline. There was no way they could land to take on survivors. Once grounded on the shingle, they would be stationary targets for the German gunners who had been practising their trade all morning. Instead they chugged slowly through the water, within range of the German guns, and trailed long ropes which the men grabbed and hung on to as they were pulled to safety.

Don scrambled into a crowded boat which scraped its way along the gravelly shore and slowly pulled away into deeper water where it could manoeuvre its way out of range of the shore batteries. He lay on the steel deck, gasping like a gaffed fish as little bloody waves of water rolled back and forth over him from the movement of the boat. All around him, wounded men and dead men stared into some imaginary distance, the wounded too stunned to grasp what was happening.

The LCA (Landing Craft Assault) was clear of the beach and was just manoeuvering to find sea room when a strafing Messerschmitt raked the craft from end to end. Don felt a blow on his foot and thought he had hit it on the side of the LCA. Suddenly, there was an ear-splitting crash, and the LCA shuddered to a dead stop in the water, hit by a shell from the shore batteries. Slowly the little craft took on a list and settled awkwardly in the water as the sea rushed in. The dead and those beyond help floated off in the oily, bloody water. Don pushed himself away from the side of the boat and looked for another landing craft, becoming slowly aware that his foot was turning numb.

Ahead of him was a big LCT. He swam towards it and grasped one of the ropes trailing from its stern as it wallowed clumsily away from the shore. Just as he had done a few minutes earlier, he flopped down on the steel deck, exhausted, amid some 50 others, many of them wounded. From the open door in the bows, some of the men kept firing at the German positions, now almost lost in the smoke of the beaches. Don looked through the door as the LCT slowly swung around providing a grim panorama of the beaches. It looked just like the newsreels he had seen of Dunkirk, but in living colour, with live sound. He was glad to be getting out of it.

The LCT moved along parallel to the beaches, gathering up survivors. They were protected by a destroyer which moved in close to the beach near them and fired back at the German batteries. As he tried to find out what was causing the numbness in his foot, Don became aware of a familiar figure beside him. His brother Vic, who had fought a few yards from him on the beach, was on the same LCT. Wearily, they exchanged greetings. They had fought near each other without realizing it, and now they were both going back to England and safety.

Things came unstuck just then. Don had found the bullet hole in his boot where the strafing plane had struck it. There was a trickle of blood, but no pain. The destroyer was running into problems of its own, having grounded close to shore under the German guns, and was trying to extricate itself. The LCT surged forward, trying to get clear of the beach area.

With a crash the LCT lurched to a sickening halt. A shore battery had found the range and sent a shell through the stern. The fuel tank went up with a loud WHOOSH, and flames spread along the boat. Dense black smoke swirled around the weary Canadians as they were forced once more back into the water. "Take care, Don!" Vic yelled as he went over the side. "You too, brother." Don replied as he leaped into the oily scum.

Don moved awkwardly in the cold, but strangely placid water. The day was a weird contrast to what was going on along the beaches. A warm sun shone in a brilliant blue sky, sparkling off the calm waters of the English Channel, thus competing with iridescent shimmers from the oil on the water. Over the beaches, the black smoke hung thick over the sad remains of the morning's disaster. Wrecked tanks stood like squat turtles, their ammunition gone, now only the targets of German batteries. Stranded LCAs and LCTs were scattered along the waters edge helplessly bobbing along the cluttered shore, still taking hits from the German guns trying to get the men taking cover inside them. Bodies lay everywhere, the dead and the wounded. They lay around the tanks, in the depressions in the sand, in the shell holes, huddled along the sea wall. Others were washed back and forth in the little waves which followed each other to the shore. Everywhere further out in the Channel, sodden khaki bundles, bobbed and rolled in the swell, most of them being carried ironically back towards the beaches they had tried to escape. Some of those shapeless khaki bundles were men still alive, desperately trying not to make themselves conspicuous targets for the snipers and machine gunners plying their trade amongst men no longer able to fight.

One of those khaki bundles lay in the water and looked cautiously around at the sound of an LCA's motor. Not far away, some brave LCA commander was still risking his life to rescue the refugees from the beaches. Ropes trailed through the water, tantalizingly near, sliding by like sea snakes as the LCA made one last effort. Don tried with all his remaining strength to reach the ropes that might lead back to England and safety. With a mighty effort, he flung himself through the water, and splashed towards the ropes. It was no use. The effort needed was now beyond him, as exhaustion and loss of blood sapped the strength he built up over all those weeks of hard training. He watched longingly as the boat slipped slowly through the water and over the horizon to England, to safety away from the bloody mess of Dieppe.

Alone, amidst the floating scum and debris of the raid, Don felt himself getting heavier as his waterlogged uniform further drained his failing strength. Wearily, he pulled off his battledress and tried to stay afloat in his underclothes. The cold water chilled his body, and he wondered how long he would last. A smoke float drifted by and he grabbed it like a providential lifebelt. It immediately turned over and headed

straight for the bottom of the Channel, with Don's hand caught in it.
With difficulty, he freed himself and popped back up like a cork to the
surface, spluttering and gasping with the effort. He quickly found
another float and grabbed it. It sank just as quickly as the first, but by
this time he learned not to grasp it in a death grip. At last, he found a
length of ship's fender rope, with large lumps of cork on it, and hung on.

The sun was now high in the sky, and starting its decline as the day
wore on. Disinterestedly, Don watched as little spurts of water erupted
here and there — snipers were trying to get the survivors in the water.
He didn't know if they were aiming deliberately for him and he didn't
care. All afternoon, he drifted down the coast, the sun shining bright
and warm on his head, the water freezing the rest of him. As he drifted
past Dieppe, bodies floated by him. Some were from his own regiment,
and one of the bodies wore a German uniform. Only one among so
many dead Canadians. An occasional kick from his weary legs kept him
from being carried too close to Dieppe. At last, when he was well clear
of the town, he let himself be carried in to shore, accompanied by
Canadian corpses gently bobbing in the quiet surf.

He had been in the water for nearly five hours. Time enough to face
the inevitability of capture. Few soldiers expect to become prisoners; it
is not part of the official plan. It is an agonizing moment; the stomach
feels knotted, the body weak, the mind confused. Up to the last moment
before capture a soldier is the worthy combatant, the adversary pressing
for advantage, then suddenly a stranger, even to himself, with hands
held high responding to commands of the enemy. A sense of bitter disappointment, anger and frustration engulfed Don as tears creased his
face — his first taste of action would be his last. What in hell went
wrong! So many young lives wasted for a few hundred feet of beach.
Don knew, as enlisted men down through the ages have known, that it
was not his job to reason why, but he certainly recognized a fouled-up
operation when it happened. Some poor bastard on the General Staff, he
thought, would have to carry the can for this one. Still the men did their
job as ordered, and under the circumstances the Canadian Second
Division had performed bravely and honourably, and there would be no
shame in capture.

His arms and knees scuffling on the rough shingle, he crawled out
of the water, half propelled by the incoming waves. He was completely
spent, shivering from the afternoon's exposure in the cold Channel, and
unable to walk. His boots were somewhere on the bottom of the
Channel along with his uniform, and his wounded foot was numb and

swollen. He sat at the foot of the cliffs and watched the bodies drift in to shore. It must have been about 7 p.m., with the sun slanting low on the horizon, when he heard German voices. Two friendly soldiers in field grey approached the near-naked wounded Canadian, chattering cheerfully as they ascertained that he was the only living soldier on the beach. Gently, they sat Don down on a kind of cradle they made by slinging their rifles between them, and carried him into Dieppe.

In the town the wounded and those not wounded were being shepherded into separate holding areas. "Are there any more of you following?" asked an anxious interpreter. "Yes, hundreds," replied Don, too weary and exasperated to care. He gathered from the conversations around him that the prisoners were all telling the same thing to their captors.

Sitting with the rest of the wounded, he suddenly realized that he was very thirsty. He hadn't had anything to drink since he had clambered into the landing craft . . . when? It seemed to have been days ago. Motioning to a passing German officer, he asked for water. The German understood, and walked over to the body of a Canadian officer. He brought back the dead officer's canteen and handed it to Don who nodded in thanks, and unscrewed the cap of the canteen. He tipped back his head and let the liquid pour down his throat. He must have swallowed half a pint before he realized the canteen was full of Navy rum. He coughed in appreciation of the pleasant surprise, and looked around the square at the huddled knots of weary and wounded soldiers, with German and French medical orderlies walking amongst them. The rum warming his belly was the first pleasant event to happen that day.

$\mathscr{C}$HAPTER $\mathscr{S}$IX

The late August darkness closed in around the long lines of men shuffling over the railway tracks at Dieppe. They wore the remnants of uniforms, and Don Errey was rather worse clad than most.

He had only his undershorts, and he shivered as he hobbled along on his wounded foot to reach the French cattle cars. He had seen the big wagons in the movies, with their "HOMMES 40 CHEVAUX 7" signs on the sides. As his wagon filled up with the weary wounded, he noted that there were considerably more than 40 men with him in the gloom, and by the look and smell of the wagon, it had played host to more than 7 horses in the very recent past.

In each mind were the questions that a prisoner-of-war asks himself: "Where are we going? What are they going to do to us?" Beyond the feelings of personal and morbid curiosity was a more basic consideration. They were all ravenous. None had eaten since the morning, many hours ago, on the assault ships.

At dawn, still in his undershorts, Don was herded out of the train with the others at Rouen. As they blinked in the pale light, they knew they were not headed for Germany, at least not now. They were pushed into German army trucks and joined a motley convoy heading for a prison hospital. Don looked under the canvas flap at the back of the truck and saw, trailing off behind, a long line of cars, army vehicles, and pushcarts loaded with the wounded from the previous morning's debacle, a slow cortege to the next stage in their lives as prisoners of the Reich.

The courtyard they entered seemed to be part of a convent or a religious institution. Some men in field gray, others in soiled khaki or remnants of underwear, milled around as vehicles were off-loaded in the yard and the wounded distributed to different sections of the main building. Inside the hospital area, they were settled on the floors of the wards and corridors, with straw for bedding. Slowly, some kind of order was resumed, as the sense of military discipline replaced the shock and disorder of the previous day. Water bottles were filled, the more seriously wounded attended to, and the corridors rang with the sounds of French-Canadian soldiers interpreting for the Anglophone Canadians and the French nurses. Food was brought in; thin porridge, soup, black bread, and some evil-smelling cheese, which even starving soldiers found hard to get into their empty bellies. While the more seriously wounded were being attended to, those like Don with less urgent needs had nothing to do but sleep. Most of them drifted off, burrowing like mice in the piles of straw, while nurses, orderlies and German guards milled about in the corridors. After the raid, capture, and the jolting journey, nothing could disturb them.

The following morning, a horde of Germans descended on the hospital — Gestapo, Wehrmacht officers, and doctors and nurses to help the few French medical personnel available. French orderlies came also, to change the bloody straw that the wounded had been lying on, and to issue water to wash the filthy survivors from the beaches. Huge thermometers were inserted into the most convenient orifices of the Canadians — Don thought they must have been meant for horses — and were left there until the doctors came to retrieve them. The thermometer in Don's posterior was the extent of his examination; his foot was left untreated, the bullet still in place.

The prisoners were interrogated by the Germans with varying degrees of skill, and little success. The ignorance of at least one questioner regarding North America was obvious. He wanted to know how long the train journey from Canada to England had lasted.

Don remained in Rouen for a week. The food improved, and the men looked forward daily to potatoes boiled in their jackets brought in steaming tubs of water to where the prisoners sprawled on the straw littering the wards and corridors. After the first day or two, with the wound in his foot still neglected, Don began to explore the building, crawling on his hands and knees, and talking to the other prisoners. Some of them had become extremely depressed in the aftermath of the raid. The hospital was full of men from the Hamilton Light Infantry, but he could find no one from the Essex Scottish.

There was little in the way of luxuries at the hospital. Like everything else, cigarettes were in short supply, and Don resorted to the Depression expedient of finding butts and rolling their contents in toilet paper. Under such circumstances these were a luxury. From one of the nurses, he scrounged a piece of cloth for a "goody bag," in which to hoard his cigarettes and bread ration. The bag, and his undershorts, were the sum total of Don Errey's possessions.

And so, with all these worldly goods, he found himself one morning at the railway station again. Still wearing only undershorts, he made the journey to Germany and a life behind barbed-wire. Those whose wounds had not been serious were herded into passenger coaches at Rouen, coaches with old-fashioned, unpadded wooden-slat seats. For nine days, frequently side-tracked for priority German transport, the train rumbled through northern France, Belgium and into Germany. As they crossed the German border a guard stuck his head into their coach and grunted laconically "Deutschland." At least the food on the train was better than that in the hospital; black bread, blood sausage, cheese and potatoes. Like all prisoners of war, everywhere and at all times, the survivors of Dieppe were learning that food was the most important thing in their lives — an obsession which would last long after they were freed.

The prisoners were ordered off the train at Kloster Haina, a small village dominated by a large church, located a short distance east of Frankfurt am Main. The regional sanitorium now had been converted to a reserve military hospital for prisoners of war. The majority of Dieppe's wounded were transferred here from Rouen. After receiving medical attention they would be sent on to a convalescent hospital further east, or to one of the large Stalags. The commandant, Dr. Zeiss, was the chief medical officer, but most of the work was handled by British medical officers captured at Dunkirk. When Don arrived there were 400 prisoners, mostly British, but with a number of French, Poles and Serbs awaiting transfer.

This hospital was luxurious in comparison to the primitive facilities at Rouen, and the treatment excellent. Hot showers, food, clothing and Red Cross parcels were welcome after the makeshift arrangements since the ceasefire on the beaches. To the British in the hospital, the Canadians brought news from outside. Apart from downed aircrews, the hospital had had few sources of news, and the Canadians, groggy from the long journey, were pumped for information by their hosts. For all the men, one anxiety was at once relieved: they were registered as prisoners by the Red Cross, and their families notified that they were still alive. Don, seeing the Red Cross in action, was impressed by their efficiency. In addition, a personal anxiety was eased — he received a uniform. After two weeks of travelling about France and Germany in his undershorts, he at last wore a well-used but serviceable British uniform.

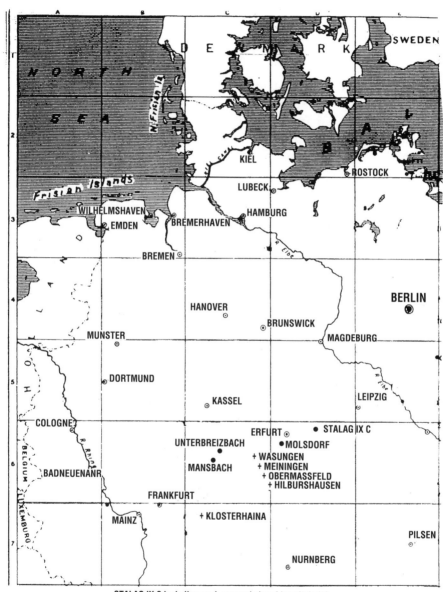

STALAG IX C including work camps (●) and hospitals (+)

As in all prisoner-of-war camps — and the hospital was still a prison — the inmates formed "combines". These were small groups established informally to share whatever the men received from home, or in their Red Cross parcels, — cigarettes, chocolate, clothing. As a member of a Canadian Scottish regiment, Don was adopted by a group of Scottish prisoners, some of whom had been POWs since Dunkirk.

There was no escape from the hospital! It was surrounded by barbed-wire and machine-gun towers, and patrolling guards served as further deterrents to escape. As new intakes of prisoners arrived, those who had recovered from their wounds left for prison camps deeper inside Germany. As each new group came in for processing Don scanned the faces in search of his brother Vic, but without success.

His foot still remained untreated and began to give him trouble. It became more painful and started to suppurate, and a German diagnosed gangrene. Don refused to have his foot amputated. He had come into the world with a foot at the end of each leg, and he planned to leave in the same condition. An Australian doctor at the hospital drained the wound and started a course of treatment. This consisted primarily of plugging the hole with gauze and draining it at three-hour intervals. It was torture, but it was worth it; the swelling went down. Eventually, Don was able to visit the physiotherapy section to exercise the ankle until it became strong enough to bear his weight. For a long time he walked with a pronounced limp.

As weeks turned into months at the hospital life settled into a routine. The prisoner-patients were counted twice a day by the guards, but otherwise left to themselves. Parcels from home, filled with cigarettes, coffee and tea, were eagerly anticipated — their contents became the prisoners' currency for bartering with the more pliable guards. The vast majority of the prisoners co-operated in their combines, producing a kind of barbed-wire socialism. A few loners refused to share, and hoarded their parcels, but they were a small minority. Some went for long though restricted walks within the hospital grounds, and others took up hobbies, but the main recreation was playing cards.

Apart from the fact that they were prisoners, life was remarkably easy: the British ran the centre competently, the medical attention was excellent, and there were no visits from the Gestapo. The prisoners got on well with the guards and with the civilian workers in the kitchens. It wasn't a holiday camp, but it was better than lying dead on the beaches of Dieppe.

In January 1943 Don, now recovered, and several other prisoners were transferred with a two-man guard to Stalag 9C - Molsdorf in Thuringia. This was a holding unit for 450 prisoners, of whom 29 were Canadians. As they marched into the camp they were once again mobbed by news-starved inmates. A surprise was in store for Don when a deep voice boomed out, "Hey Errey, you lost again." The booming voice belonged to Pat Murphy, a boyhood friend from Wallaceburg who served in the same platoon as Vic. Pat could only confirm what Don already knew, that Vic had succeeded in reaching one of the landing craft. Don did learn that the majority of the Canadians taken at Dieppe were confined in one of the many camps administered as Stalag 9C. If Vic were alive, chances were that he would be in one of these camps. There was only one thing for Don to do — get transferred from camp to camp within Stalag 9C until he found his brother. But for the moment Don had a more pressing problem — his own survival.

Molsdorf was a brutal change from the hospital. The International Red Cross repeatedly petitioned the German authorities regarding conditions in this camp. Each hut housed more than eighty men in double-tiered bunks and was heated by a pot-bellied stove at either end. Most of the men were prisoners from Dunkirk, and many were sick and depressed from years of captivity. Several committed suicide. As in the hospital, they were counted twice a day, with additional searches and inspections whenever the Germans decreed. Every half hour during daylight, and often at night, the loudspeakers would blare news of fresh German victories to the weary prisoners.

Each day the men were marched off in groups to work in the potato fields. For this they were paid in Kriegsgefangene money, but more valuable than currency were the potatoes they lifted from the fields and stuffed into their tunics. The guards usually turned a blind eye to this theft from the Reich, but there were unsporting types who searched the prisoners on their return in the evening. The prisoners circumvented these eagle-eyed inspectors by tossing the spuds over the barbed-wire as they marched to the gate, where they were collected by the men inside.

The guards at Stalag 9C were tougher than those assigned to the prison hospital, the roughest being those who had served on the Russian front. They considered the prisoners to be enjoying a soft life, while they who had suffered the rigours of the East were due to be returned there. When parcels from home and the Red Cross arrived their anger would increase, as they saw the prisoners receiving luxuries denied them; tea, coffee and cigarettes — above all cigarettes. These the prisoners used as bribes and currency, as they were far superior to the miserable weeds which passed for cigarettes in the German Army. Eventually the German authorities totally controlled the Red Cross food parcels and prisoners were issued only two tins daily.

Time passed slowly at Molsdorf. The men grew beards and mustaches, and kept boredom at bay by playing cards or volleyball, walking round the perimeter, or trying to escape. Escape was usually hopeless from the start. There were few trees around the camp which was set in a featureless plain: any break through the wire would be noticed immediately, and exit points for tunnels would be easily detected as well. Still, they tried. Escape committees were formed, tunnels were dug, documents were forged, and uniforms were dyed to look like civilian clothes. Dyes were made from the boiled covers of books received through the Red Cross.

Don and his fellow Commonwealth prisoners were used as dirt-dumpers by the tunnelers, surreptitiously getting rid of the earth dug up by the "moles" trying to get through the camp perimeters. A successful break from the camp was never made during Don's stay, but the activity kept hope alive, and provided a relief from the constant irritation of blaring loudspeakers, sudden searches, visits from Gestapo interrogators, and the thousand petty restrictions placed on the men. After each escape attempt, stiffer restrictions were imposed on the whole camp, the most onerous being the termination of all outdoor recreation.

The men looked forward to mealtimes, and established their own standard of gourmet delicacies — such as slabs of hardtack soaked in water overnight and fried for breakfast in the morning. They were permitted to keep salt in the huts, but pepper and hot mustard were "verboten" because they could be used to blind guards in escape attempts. For the hundreds of Britons, Canadians, New Zealanders, Australians and South Africans in the camp, one day followed another with little variation. Reveille at seven, roll call and inspection, work in the fields for those able to work, cards, sports, walking the barbed-wire perimeters, letters from home (censored by camp authorities) inspection and lights out at 10 p.m.

It wasn't much of a life, and Don wanted a change.

CHAPTER SEVEN

By spring of 1943, Don felt it was time to move on, but how? There was no conceivable way out over the wire or under it. The only way was through the main gate. Perhaps with a little ingenuity he could outwit his captors.

As a youth, he had suffered and recovered from jaundice. With the aid of a sympathetic South African doctor, he decided to mimic the symptoms, and succeeded in persuading the camp authorities that he might have yellow fever. He was taken under two-man escort to a prison hospital at Wasungen. There he presented a letter from the South African doctor to the British M.O. in charge. With a wink to Don, he had him put in a private room with all the books and Red Cross parcels he could wish for. This, Don concluded, was the way to see out the war.

In fact, the hospital, a converted factory, was a grim spot. The majority of the 325 prisoners were Belgians, Poles and Russians. Many were suffering skin diseases contracted during spells of forced labour in the salt mines. The Russians in particular were treated like animals, and many died every day. Starved by the Germans, the treatment given them by the Commonwealth doctors at the hospital was of little avail. Every morning Don watched from his window as bodies were dumped at the railroad track beside the hospital to await disposal.

In view of the barbarous treatment extended by Russians and Germans to each other, many preferred death to capture. During the Crimean War of 1854-6 widespread concern was generated in Europe over the extreme deprivation suffered by soldiers. In 1864 the Geneva Convention led to the establishment of the International Red Cross, and a code of conduct to civilize the behaviour of states at war. The Convention did much during subsequent conflicts to reduce the barbarity; Russia, however, refused to become a signatory of the Convention. As a result the Germans and Russians were not legally bound by this

International Code of behaviour, and their mutual acts of brutality were limited only by their ingenuity.

Don witnessed this brutal treatment of the Russians, and had difficulty reconciling it with his comparative comfort. He would never forget what he saw at Wasungen. The risk of death had lessened dramatically for him following Dieppe, not so for the Russians.

After a month in isolation Don began to hope for repatriation through the Red Cross. X-rays showed a spot on his liver, a relic of his bout with jaundice, but it was not sufficiently abnormal to convince the German doctors, who had the final word on repatriation. In desperation he persuaded the British doctors to say they suspected diphtheria, and wished to keep him under observation for a further two weeks. The reply of the German medics was simple and unambiguous, — Don was up-ended on his bed and injected with a massive, and excruciating shot of diphtheria vaccine. Where the Germans were concerned he was a healthy prisoner, and ready to do his bit for the Reich. At his next location he would have to work for a living.

The next stop was Hilberghausen, a little village right out of Grimm's Fairy Tales; houses with steep pitched roofs and carved balconies, cobblestones on the streets, and a tinkling fountain in the village square. Again, this seemed a good place to spend the war, in a well-run hospital staffed by British medics. It was safely separated by barbed-wire from "The Nuthouse" across the road where Nazi doctors were suspected of conducting experiments on the mentally ill. For the moment, however, spring was in the air, and the high, wooded hills of Thuringia were a reminder that neutral Switzerland was nearby, if there were a way to escape.

The prison hospital was an informal place despite the barbed-wire and the ever-present guards. It didn't take Don long to find out that he could slip into the village beer-houses for a quick one without difficulty. One of the prisoners was detailed to pick up the mail at the village post office using a small two-wheeled cart to carry letters and parcels back to camp. Don convinced a guard — using a tin of cocoa for persuasion — that he should go along to exercise his foot. The exercise usually took several hours. The prisoners became well-known to the villagers, who greeted them on their excursions to the post office as if they were old inhabitants. During their tours of Hilberghausen, they would go to the back of the beer halls and quaff a few liters of weak beer in exchange for cigarettes, the favoured currency for prisoners of war. Given the tranquillity and natural beauty of the village it was at times difficult to remember that a war was going on, and this suited the prisoners well. There were few soldiers to be seen, other than the hospital guards. The town had no war industries, and was far enough away from the industrial heart of Germany to be off the usual bomber routes into the country.

Eventually Don became fit enough to work, and was transferred back to Molsdorf for assignment to a work camp. He was sent to Stalag 9C - Mansbach. The prisoners called it S-camp. Officially designated "Sonderlager", or special camp, it was for prisoners who had attempted one or more escapes from other camps. Perhaps the Germans in checking Don's records were becoming suspicious of his actions. In less than one year of prison life he had already been in and out of four camps. Don continued to give them good reason to suspect him.

Mansbach was a work camp which provided labourers for a nearby stone quarry. The twenty-eight prisoners lived in one large barrack block with double-tiered bunks. Every morning, Monday through Saturday, the men were awakened at 4:30, fed and marched off at 5:15 under armed escort to the quarry, 3 miles away. Work commenced at 6:30. If the prisoners filled the stipulated number of wagons with rocks they returned to camp at 5:30 p.m. If not, they stayed until the task was done. At the quarry, which was really a mountain under demolition, the prisoners worked beside civilian labourers. On arrival at the quarry, they were issued with a pick, shovel, crowbar, and two different sizes of sledgehammer. They were also issued numbered brass tags — after breaking huge rocks into small stones and loading them into buggies, the men attached their tags to the buggies to show who had done the work. The buggies were then sent down the hill on a cable to the stone crusher machines, where the stones were reduced to gravel.

Needless to say, the performance of the prisoners fell short of the high standards set by their civilian counterparts. This was due in part to a general lack of skill among the prisoners, but also an unwillingness to be useful to the Reich. Like his comrades, Don worked competently when he was being watched, and did everything wrong when the foreman's back was turned. A friend of Don's, Tiny Sinclair of the Royal Hamilton Light Infantry, was perhaps the most disruptive worker in the camp. His favorite trick was to break the rocks into pieces which were just too large for the crushers to handle, load them on the buggies, cover them with smaller pieces and finally attaching a tag stolen from the civilians. When these rocks reached the crushers, they usually brought the huge machines to a grinding halt. Some unsuspecting civilian would then be hauled into the main office at the bottom of the hill for a reprimand.

On one occasion Tiny Sinclair, in a fit of temper, fought with a guard, and wrestled his rifle from him. He was about to throw it over the edge of the cliff when the guard burst into tears. Sinclair relented and returned the weapon. As Don later commented, "this kind of guard was few and far between," — in most camps, Sinclair would have been shot.

Under the Geneva Convention work parties (Arbeitskommandos) were permitted, provided they were used for non-military purposes. The work camps offered many advantages. The prisoners were usually better fed and quartered in the interest of making them into effective workers. They naturally had greater freedom of movement as they left camp each day to work side by side with civilian labourers. This was particularly important to prisoners who suffered "camp fever", and for whom the daily experience of living behind barbed-wire took its toll. But Don and many others liked the work camp because it offered the best opportunities for escape. Security was less strict, the barbed-wire fencing less effective, and the guards were usually more compliant and fewer in number. There was, however, one great disadvantage. In a main camp there existed a large pool of talent for the escape committee. Clothing could be dyed and tailored, various identity, work and travel documents forged, and currency obtained. In a small work camp these important items were almost impossible to acquire. Although escape might be easier, without a reasonable survival kit recapture was almost inevitable. Don learned this the hard way.

At the quarry, security was lax. The guards reasoned correctly that a POW wearing an allied uniform would not get very far. Don felt it was his duty to make the attempt, and that even a few hours freedom would be worth the risk. Perhaps, more importantly, it would boost his morale. Although a prisoner, he was still a part of the Allies' war effort — escape seemed the best way to express this.

There were no toilet facilities available at the quarry for the POWs. The usual procedure was to signal a nearby guard and retreat to a handy bush. Don signalled his intention and hurried off to a large clump of bushes, passed them, and kept on walking. He expected to hear the guttural command "Achtung" but no one paid any attention to him. When he reached the security of a large wood, he sat down under a tree, rested his back against the trunk, lit a cigarette and savoured his freedom. The guards would surely be on top of him in a minute or two. After twenty minutes of relaxation he realized that the guard must have forgotten about him. He pressed on through the wood down a hillside and into a farming area. He was noticed at a distance by a couple of farm hands. Don waved and they, intent on their labour, merely waved back. In a burst of hope he headed southward, thinking he might make it all the way to Switzerland. Reality soon dispelled such fantasy. He carelessly ventured too close to a dirt road. Two villagers returning from the fields spotted Don and beckoned for him to come. There was nothing to do but respond, and the villagers returned him to the quarry. What infuriated him most was not the returning to camp but the bruise to his ego. Back at the quarry it was clear that he had not even been missed, and no alarm had been sounded! Don had been gone for less than three hours but it felt good.

The food ration at Mansbach was better than in many prison camps. Lunch consisted of black bread, blood sausage or cheese, cabbage and horsemeat. On one occasion, the prisoners helped themselves from a steaming kettle of soup, with chunks of meat floating in it. After agreeing that it was one of the better meals in their time as workers for the Reich, Don stirred the pot and the ladle caught on something at the bottom. Carefully, he lifted a heavy mass. As it broke the surface it was recognizable as a horse's skull, with scraps of meat still adhering. The boiled eyes, protruding, stared accusingly at the suddenly nauseated prisoners.

Good as their meals were, the men felt something was missing. They began to distill their own supply of alcohol using an old sauerkraut barrel and copper tubing from the stone plant. They were able to produce an indescribable but undeniably potent concoction from dried raisins and apricots. The elixir was produced in a 10-day cycle, and consumed in a fraction of that time at weekend drinking sessions. These often became rowdy, but the guards, bribed with the chocolate, tea and cigarettes, did not intervene. The guards gained something else as well — the prisoners were usually easier to handle.

Because the camp was surrounded by forest, the prisoners could do extra work on the weekends cutting wood. Their overseer was a Forest Ranger who always wore his colorful costume while superintending their labors. They were fed at his house and became friendly with the Ranger's family, especially the little daughter, Idletraut, who was teased by the men after they let her know that her name meant "lazy fish" in English. The food was the main attraction of the weekend work. The Ranger's wife was an excellent cook, and would often bake white bread for the men to take back to camp. In wartime any kind of white bread was a luxury.

Eventually the desire for freedom was again too much for Don to resist, and a convenient, if unsanitary, escape route presented itself. The camp latrine stood beside the barbed-wire perimeter, and a small flap at the back of the structure allowed access for the local honey wagon to retrieve the contents for use on surrounding farms. Many prisoners felt this was an appropriate gift to the Reich. Each day, while the men were working at the quarry, a local farmer would come and methodically draw off the fragrant treasure. Each evening, just as methodically, one of the prisoners would check the flap. This manoeuvre, risky to work boots, required a great deal of gymnastic ability. The "pit" ran the length of the latrine along the back wall. In front stood a low wooden wall and over the middle of the pit, running the entire length was the "roost" pole. By stepping over the short wooden wall and ducking under the "roost" pole it was possible to balance on two parallel two-by-fours located half way down the pit, and test the flap. One evening Don took his turn. It had not been properly latched and opened easily. He returned to the compound, notching his belt as he did so for the benefit of any suspicious onlookers. Two Scots who had been captives since Dunkirk quickly agreed to escape with Don. In a small camp of thirty prisoners any more than three would be readily missed. Beginning at seven o'clock that evening a steady, but not unusual, number of men made their way to the latrine. By nine o'clock a sufficient number had entered so that none of the guards noticed when three fewer men exited. Don and his chums hid until eleven o'clock. The men in the barracks were feigning sleep too well Don thought. The only sounds were the footfalls and occasional cough of passing guards. The men knew that the guard who paced the perimeter of the camp passed the back of the latrine approximately once every thirty minutes. After hearing his retreating footsteps one of the Scots volunteered to go first and gingerly balanced on the two-by-fours and successfully rolled out through the flap. Don was next and executed the manoeuvre with near perfection. However he thought he heard a cracking sound as he rolled out. Lying in the darkness provided by the shadow of the latrine they waited nervously for their comrade. From within the latrine they heard a louder cracking sound and a barely audible word spoken in the soft burr of the Scot - "shit". The two-by-four had given way and their chum was up to his waist in the Reich's night soil. He dare not move for fear the noise had alerted the guards and so he waited. After a few minutes had elapsed and no one had come to investigate, he rolled out through the flap.

The trio raced into a nearby woods finding it difficult to breathe without gagging and, for two of them, without laughing. Fortunately they found a stream, into which their more pungent colleague was precipitately dunked until the worst of the stench had gone. They walked all night and were soaked by a constant series of downpours. At midday they came to the edge of the woods. The forest had given way to a series of wheat fields. They debated their situation. They had not put many miles between themselves and the camp. A decision was reached: they would risk crossing the field in daylight rather than wait for nightfall. Crouching low they entered the wheat field and crept diagonally toward the woods on the far side. Mid-way across the field they walked into a small knot of farm workers! They couldn't be seen from the woods as they had made a clearing in the middle of the field and were resting out of sight of the farm owner. With great aplomb the trio bade the group an enthusiastic good-day in passable German, and continued on their way. But not for long. They turned at the sound of running feet and found themselves staring at a forest of sharp pitchforks. They surrendered.

Their punishment was not severe. Rations were cut back for three days and the guards thought the whole episode amusing. Although they didn't know it, the prisoners were due to be transferred anyway. The next stop for Don was the salt mines, a brief and destructive excursion into the nether regions of the Reich's wartime economy.

CHAPTER EIGHT

Word was received to move out of Mansbach, and Don gathered his collection of pipes and few belongings and marched with the other prisoners to Unterbreizbach, about 10 miles away. It was indicative of how the war was going that their place in the camp was taken by prisoners from Italy, a nation now divided against itself.

They arrived at Unterbreizbach late at night. The new camp was next to the huge salt mine complex where they were to work. The camp had existed since 1940 and contained about 150 men. In addition to the British there were seven or eight Australians, New Zealanders and South Africans. Tiny Sinclair and Don doubled the Canadian Contingent. The prisoners were housed in wooden barracks with sixteen men to a room on two-tiered bunks. There was an infirmary and a room for theatrical performances, which doubled as a games room. There was no sports ground, but the men were often taken to swim in a nearby river.

A major concern of the POWs was the food. It was prepared in a kitchen outside the camp by a civilian chef, and was so bad the prisoners threatened to strike. They learned to predict the arrival of the International Red Cross inspectors because their food improved dramatically two days before each visit, and returned to its usual grim state afterwards. Petitions by the senior NCO and the Red Cross inspector brought little improvement.

The men were divided into four groups for work. One group worked underground for eight to nine hours daily, while a second worked at the surface for nine to ten hours. Another shift would take over at the completion of the first. Usually a prisoner would have one Sunday off in every four.

On his first day at the mine, Don, like the other prisoners, was issued a time card which had to be punched each morning on beginning work, and each evening on finishing. As their first act of sabotage, the prisoners jammed their cards down the machine making it unusable. The Germans quickly saw through the game, and thereafter a guard would take the cards and punch them in one by one.

The mine was reached after a long journey in an open boxcar down a Stygian shaft. Before descending prisoners were told to yell when the pressure built up in their ears. Nothing had prepared Don for what ensued. As they descended into the gloom the car gathered speed until he was sure the cable supporting them must have broken. Faster and faster they plummetted, the black walls of the shaft racing past like a blur. As the pressure grew intolerable the car's occupants let out a bloodcurdling scream, Don thought his last moment had come. It was more frightening than anything that had happened to him on the Dieppe beaches.

At last the car slowed abruptly and came to a halt at the bottom of the shaft. The men got out. They saw something none of them could have imagined. Instead of a series of dimly-lit tunnels the mine resembled an underground city, the main tunnel nearly one quarter of a mile wide, dazzlingly lit by strings of electric lights. A roadway, miniature rail lines, and street lights, made it look like a brightly-illuminated railway terminus. Everywhere little cars, bicycles, and motorcycles carried workmen to their assigned areas. The men took in this astonishing sight, like a scene from an updated Wagnerian opera, before they were quickly hustled off to their work areas. Don was assigned to work about five miles from the main shaft. Bicycles were used for transportation, but, since none were left , Don started to walk and had gone two miles before someone on a motorcycle stopped to pick him up and carry him the rest of the way.

It was the beginning of an enjoyably destructive episode in his career as a prisoner. That first day, he was assigned to a crew replacing sections of the miniature railway tracks. The heavy rails were each carried by three men, and Don found that all his workmates were German civilians. As the shortest of the crew, he was placed in the centre when they carried the rails, and he found it simple to gradually wriggle himself into a lower position so that the entire load was carried by the men at the front and rear, while he gave a theatrical display of puffing and struggling with the rail section balanced one millimetre above his shoulder. The suspicions of the other two men mounted until at last Don decided to cease the subtle deception, and stepped from under the rail, moved to one side and lit up a cigarette. He then moved beside the workers sweating under the steel rail and chatted amiably about work in the salt mines. There was nothing the other two could do: dropping the rail and forcing the "Dummkopf Kanadischer" to do his share would simply mean another struggle to pick the thing up again. In silent rage they continued their journey through the tunnel as Don filled the air with the fragrance of Sweet Caps, and chattered on about the chances of the Detroit Red Wings winning the Stanley Cup next year. The Germans ignored him for the rest of the day. Next morning when he showed up at the work area, they simply looked at him and said "nein," to their foreman.

Unperturbed by his unpopularity, Don was put in another crew, this time loading rock salt on to empty cars near the main face of the mine. The workers, who were on a profitable bonus scheme, sweated like slaves to keep the cars loaded and running in long strings to the main shipment areas. As the cars reached the workers, they were stopped by the simple expedient of placing a 2x4 plank in front of the wheels to prevent them rolling beyond the loading area. Don pretended he couldn't get the hang of it and managed to overturn most of the cars which came his way. As the day wore on, he became most unpopular with the rest of the crew, who saw their bonuses evaporating like snow in the desert, whatever their thoughts may have been about patriotic contributions to the war effort.

In truth, Don didn't much like the salt mine. There was some air conditioning, but the atmosphere of the place was a fetid approximation of hell. The air was stale, and everything smelled the same, and the food tasted the same because of the salt everywhere in the air. There were grimmer sights too, which contributed to the Hades-like atmosphere of the place. The mine employed Russians as slave labor, many of whom were women. They were all on starvation rations, and the Germans considered them expendable. From time to time the other prisoners would surreptitiously slip them tins of cocoa and chocolate, but the odds were against their long-term survival. There was little more Don and his comrades could do to help. Don watched one day as a German worker kicked a Russian woman who had collapsed beside one of the tracks. She was pregnant, and the violent blow started her labor. Don was quickly hustled away from the scene, so never found out what happened to the woman.

Not long after he began work in the mine he was called into the main office, instead of into the time punch area. The camp interpreter stood there with several grim-faced officials from the mine. The interpreter cleared his throat:

"I don't know what kind of trouble you're trying to cause down there.

I know you don't want to work here in Germany any more than I'd want to work in Canada, but they don't want you down below any more."

Having been booted out of the mine, Don was sent to the machine shop above ground. On the first day he was put to work on a drill press, putting holes in lengths of cut pipe. Before the first morning passed, he had broken three hardened steel bits. Once more he was out of a job.

The Germans gave him one more chance. A foreman stood over him as Don was put in charge of a chopping machine which cut lengths of metal suitable for use as chisels at the face of the salt mine. Don quickly proved himself adept in this complex art, cutting the metal strips to within a fraction of a millimetre of the required length. Satisfied at last, the foreman left. Somehow, Don's skill deteriorated rapidly without the supervision of the foreman. Some of the metal strips came out 3 inches long, some 3 feet long, and there were many creative variations in length in between. Sometime late in the afternoon, a shadow fell across Don.

"Dummkopf Kanadischer!" came the foreman's enraged screech.

A guard was set to escort the saboteur back to the camp. Don was brought before the commandant.

"From the telephone calls we have received from the mine, they don't want you back — ever."

Don was placed where he could do no further harm to the Reich economy, cleaning up the camp and peeling potatoes in the kitchen. It was a lot better than working in the mine.

Things fell into a not unpleasant routine. After cleaning the camp area and doing his chores in the kitchen, Don spent his evenings as the camp's gambling boss. He started a casino, to the delight of everyone including the guards, and his talent for improvisation was given free rein. Two Crown and Anchor games fashioned from pieces of plywood were rotated on spikes nailed to the barracks walls, and empty Red Cross boxes were fashioned into an Odds and Evens numbers game. But the favourite of the betting crowd were the evening horse races. Don constructed a race track from cardboard boxes measuring sixteen feet long by eight feet wide. The track was divided into 78 squares from start to finish line. Six outline horses were cut from the cardboard and crayoned in different colours, then mounted on four-inch wooden bases. A deck of cards was altered — the playing surfaces now bore the colours of the horses and new numbers — to provide the motive power for the sport of kings. Each evening the race announcer would shuffle the deck, pull out the first card and the race would commence, with commentary by the announcer. It wasn't Ascot, or even Greenwood, but that did not deter the gamblers. The odds were usually never higher than three to one, and a horse could be handicapped by removing one or more of its cards from the deck before the race. A disc bearing the colour of the horse would be purchased before post time — cigarettes, not money being the currency of the camp. Thus, with no government meddling in their economic affairs, the POW camps were probably — in miniature — the only market economies in the world operating strictly by the laws of supply and demand. The market value of a cigarette could fluctuate wildly, according to the most recent arrival of the Red Cross packages.

Don was reaching the height of his powers as the camps most adept scrounger, and the man to whom prisoners went if they wanted to exchange one commodity for another. His next move, by popular demand, was to open a swap shop. Since cigarettes were the gold standard of the barbed-wire economy — each day the current rate of exchange was assessed in terms of cigarettes and posted on the notice board, along with the shop's hours of business. Any hard feelings about the heartless banking establishment were prevented by Don's insistence that each player take a turn as a camp banker.

As well as gambling and commodity markets, entertainment became a camp industry. Music was provided for the casino when a British lance corporal from Birmingham formed a band. It wasn't quite Glenn Miller, but, like the race track, it was their own. To top off an evening's entertainment drinks were available, courtesy of several carefully-chosen and well-bribed guards. Given the circumstances, the prisoners of the Reich managed to divert themselves quite nicely.

Even running the camp's entertainment affairs eventually lost it's diversionary effect. Don was still a prisoner, and still at the mercy of inspections, guards, and all the dreary routines dictated by his captors. It was time for a change. Don decided to take advantage of the spot on his liver. He wanted to leave camp and to look for his brother again. But, unknown to him as yet, he was also going to be busier than he had ever been in his life behind barbed-wire. This time he was going to work, not for the Germans, but for his own people, and at German expense.

CHAPTER NINE

Once the war began to turn against the Germans, it became easier to bribe those guards who could envisage a possible role reversal in the near future. Don had little difficulty talking his way out of Unterbreizbach. He told a friendly guard that he wanted to look for his brother, and that he had a plausible excuse if only he could find an accommodating doctor. The guard knew of one in town, and for two tins of cocoa Don arranged to see the good doctor. One tin rewarded the guard, the other paid the doctor. Don found him to be an amiable type, eager to talk about his family and forget about the war. Don spent a day with him while the doctor prodded in a perfunctory fashion at the wiry Canadian. Don was pronounced unfit to work in the salt mines, or anywhere else. This, of course, only confirmed what his German workmates had already learned, but for other reasons.

Clutching the official-looking piece of paper which testified to the near-disintegration of his liver, Don returned to the camp. He presented the medical assessment to the camp Commandant. Don thought he detected a sigh of relief from the Commandant as he signed the papers ordering Don's transfer to the prison hospital at Obermassfeld.

In February 1944, Don was escorted through the gates at Obermassfeld. He presented his documents to the British doctors, who acknowledged that Don must surely be at death's door, and would have to spend the next while as a bed patient, waited on hand and foot, with good food and the best treatment circumstances could afford. After a few days of this wise treatment, Don came to the unshakeable conclusion that it should continue to the end of the war.

After one week, however, he became bored. Even the most self-indulgent appetite becomes sated when there is little to break the monotony of eating and sleeping. Don found himself wandering the corridors of the hospital, chatting with the prisoners, and exploring the camp.

Once a factory, then a Hitler Youth Centre, the camp now served as an orthopedic centre for Allied prisoners-of-war. Obermassfeld reflected the changing nature of the war as an increasing number of the prisoners were Americans. The number of downed American flyers rose as the Americans increased their massive daylight bombing raids on the German industrial centres. Over half of the 480 patients at Obermassfeld were U.S. aircrew. Amongst all the twanging North American accents, Don heard one or two familiar strains. The Royal Canadian Air Force also was contributing prisoners to the hospital as German defences took their toll of bomber crews in the British night raid campaigns. The Germans were having great difficulty providing sufficient hospital space, and Obermassfeld was becoming overcrowded.

Most of the patients were severely wounded amputees, suffering from extensive burns in addition to shrapnel wounds which often became infected. A ten-man team of British Medical Officers under Major J. Sherman and chief surgeon Major Kimbell provided excellent medical care in spite of limited facilities. A physiotherapy program for amputees had been introduced, but many who returned to physical health remained mentally depressed as they visualized their post-war existence dealing with an handicap

An RCAF Flying Officer, E.F. Haddlesey, DFC, of Norwood, Ontario, refused to become depressed. He had lost a leg, but was determined not to go through life on crutches. Each day he went to the workshop of the Camp shoemaker, "Chukka" MacKinnon, where he attempted to construct an artificial limb, but without success. Frustrated by this he decided to give up and wait for early repatriation. It was then that he met Don. Impulsively Don offered to build him an artificial leg.

"You mean that?" said the flyer.

"Yeah, sure," Don answered, "won't be anything complicated," then hurried away to find out about artificial limbs. As a youth Don discovered he had a natural talent for creative crafts of all kinds — especially items fashioned from wood. As a Boy Scout he had won numerous awards for his craftsmanship. An artificial limb was another matter.

His first stop was also at shoemaker MacKinnon, a Highlander taken in the bag at Dunkirk, who listened as Don told him what he had let himself in for. "Aye," he said, "Ye"ll hae tae use something for the foot," and brought out a wooden shoe lath.

Don took the lath and started to work. Measurements of the stump were taken, doctors were consulted as to pressures, fittings, and materials, other prisoners lent their expertise as Don developed his skills in metal working, wood-carving, leather cutting and perfected his talent for scrounging. A tin of cocoa passed to the right guard would bring much needed rubber, rivets, or small pieces of metal.

Don tried everything to make the leg work. The cup for the stump was fashioned from hard leather which MacKinnon used for the soles of shoes. This was pounded with heavy wooden mallets until it was soft enough to shape. Several components were made from pieces of window frames and metal chairs. In a short time the whole hospital was engaged in the epic of Haddlesey's leg. Through much experimenting, Haddlesey was an eager and patient subject.

By trial and error Don was able to solve the main problems of constructing a successful artificial limb. The weight of the limb was borne by the shoulders. Straps attached to the prosthesis passed over each shoulder through a belt at the waist and were reattached to the front of the limb. A more serious problem was the articulation of the foot. In walking, the heel strikes the surface first, and the foot then rocks on to the toes. In preparation for the next step the foot is slightly raised, the heel goes down and the toes up. This becomes an automatic reflex action, and once someone learns how to walk he no longer has to think about it. How then to design pieces of wood and metal in the form of an artificial limb which will execute this unconscious yet highly complicated manoeuvre? After a great deal of thought, experimentation, and even greater patience by Haddlesey, the solution was discovered. By attaching a semi-circular piece of rubber from an old tire to the front of the shoe lath, a crude but functional substitute for the toes was formed. Rubber bands attached above the articulation that served as the knee, and inserted into the instep area of the shoe lath, raised the front part of the foot putting the heel in proper position for the next step. The weight of the body when applied to the heel created the rocking forward motion onto the rubber toe, and the process would then be repeated.

The final obstacle was the one which caused the greatest pain — the fit of the stump into the cup. Cotton batting was used in the leather cup to form a close fit around the stump. Any movement within the cup would cause chafing of the skin. Gradually the skin around the stump would thicken and become calloused and the constant packing of the cotton would create a perfect fit. Haddlesey and Don were two very proud men on the day that the flyer walked across the compound with hardly a limp and no pain. Initially Don saw the challenge as a means of occupying his time and helping a Canadian buddy. Once the artificial limb had been completed he planned to find another diversion. But it was not to be: he was launched on a new career, that lasted until the war ended. If he could provide a leg for one flyer why not for others. Could he make an artificial arm? What about raised arm splints? Don had found his niche, and he embraced the opportunity whole-heartedly. The life of a prisoner now took on meaning. Don's creative talent and abundant energy, which had found their outlet in destructive acts and playful activities, were now channeled into constructive and humanitarian efforts.

The British doctors in charge of the hospital saw the enterprise as tremendous therapy for the patients. The men who had lost the use of one leg, or both, could look forward to regaining their mobility: those who still had the use of their limbs could feel that they were doing something useful for their more seriously-wounded comrades. The Germans even co-operated by allowing Don and MacKinnon to take over a stor-

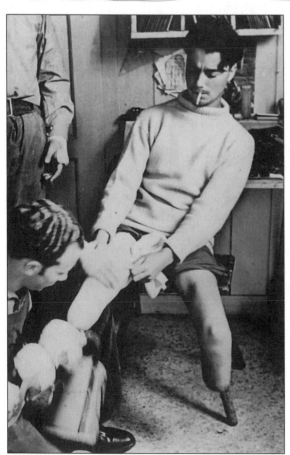

Don (left) and Sgt. R. (Salty) Salt in one of the innumerable fittings. A triumph of will and courage.

Don at work in the Mieningen prison hospital. In the background his colleague Sgt. R. Scott.

age shed for their flourishing artificial leg enterprise.

Don experimented constantly with new materials and new techniques, and he brought the arts of bribery and scrounging to new heights as he enlisted the aid of guards in finding scarce materials. He tried different systems of articulation for joints, and experimented with a variety of splints in an attempt to get balky limbs functioning once more.

In an attempt to ease the overcrowding in the camp the Germans opened a new prison hospital on May 14, 1944. Located five kilometres away in the town of Mieningen, it served as a convalescent hospital for amputees from Obermassfeld. In late June Don was transferred to Mieningen and was provided with a decently-equipped workshop and several assistants.

The hospital had been originally an opera house, then a German Reserve hospital, and now an orthopaedic centre. The Senior British Medical Officer was Capt. J.E. Wooding, and the Senior American

Officer, Major James C. Evans, United States Army Air Force. This camp also became overcrowded. More than half of the 472 prisoners were American. As the Allies slowly made gains following the successful D-Day assault, the numbers of captured aircrews increased. Don and his assistants were kept very busy.

The principal structure in the camp was the three-storey opera house set in a large courtyard. Behind this stood four large huts and, for a short time, an Allied field hospital captured near Arnhem. The amphitheatre of the main building had been turned into a general ward for fifty men. A section of the lobby had been enclosed to house Don's workshop.

His first assistant was a British flyer, Sgt. Scott (Scotty). Scotty's arm and shoulder had been badly crushed when his bomber had been shot down. Don developed a raised arm splint which kept the arm elevated at the shoulder level while the bones healed. Over time the splint was lowered until a simple hand cast sufficed. Once on the mend, Scotty volunteered to help with the amputees. Another recruit was M/Sgt. Matt Kraemer, USAAF, from Battle Creek, Michigan. Matt had his right leg amputated and was walking on a new leg which Don had fashioned. Kraemer became a welcome addition to the flourishing workshop. As the war continued many amputees were repatriated and Don lost his assistants. Volunteers quickly replaced them. Two new assistants who stayed until the war ended were Privates Ron Perry and Jack Faulkner, both members of Highland regiments taken at Dunkirk.

Don continued to improve the design and efficiency of his handcrafted prostheses. He developed a special splint for men with injured Achilles tendons. Where previously those afflicted used to hobble around with their heels flopping uselessly, they walked normally, thanks to Don's unpatented spring-based drop foot splint. As the improvements grew so did Don's confidence, and confidence was essential as he undertook an exceedingly difficult challenge. Sgt. R. Salt, an RAF bomb aimer in a Lancaster squadron, had lost both legs. When his plane was hit he parachuted out the bomb bay doors. The plane lurched as Salty jumped and the doors slammed shut crushing his legs just below the knees. Fortunately he was immediately picked up and taken directly to a military hospital. Following surgery he was sent to Meiningen for convalescence and Physiotherapy. Each morning his mates would pick him up and take him outside. He would sit quietly talking to others until meal time when his mates would pick him up and take him back inside.

Salty appreciated the assistance but detested being so dependent. He wanted legs.

Some of the prisoners were anxious about Salty's determination to walk. The amputees who had lost one leg had had difficulty in learning to walk on an artificial one. Balancing on two artificial limbs seemed impossible. The weight of the body would rest totally on the leg stumps where they were supported on the cups of the prostheses. The pain would be excruciating and chafing of the stumps a certainty. But Salty was determined. If Squadron-Leader Douglas Bader could command a squadron on two tin legs, Sgt. R. Salt would walk.

Don decided to accept the challenge the evening Salty declared in jest, "If you make me a pair of legs I'll have the first dance on New Years Eve." Innumerable fittings were made to achieve the close fit between stump and cup and extra padding inserted to ease the discomfort, but nothing could prevent the initial chafing. Salty's leg stumps were rubbed raw. But he refused to give up. Eventually the stumps became calloused and with the aid of canes Salty regained his mobility and his independence. On New Year's Eve, 1944, he danced and strutted about the camp without canes. Many of the prisoners, Don included, wept openly at this triumph of will and raw courage.

There were many side benefits that Don enjoyed in his new career. He needed large amounts of cotton batting which the Red Cross supplied. Ordinarily cotton batting has little value, but in war-ravaged Germany it provided Don considerable scrounging power. The Camp administration hired local women as secretaries. Feminine hygiene accessories were in extremely short supply, so cotton batting was used as a substitute for sanitary napkins. Don became the Camp's most sought after benefactor! Through this contact with the civilian staff Don was able to purchase a radio, one part at a time. A good friend, Flying Officer Bob Kost of Toronto, reassembled the pieces. Bob was a medical student studying in England when war broke out. Early in the war he was shot down in a Blenheim bomber. Although uninjured, he managed to be sent to a prison hospital where he was able to intern. Bob had a room on the third floor of the main building where the radio was hidden. He had an old desk with a box built on top fronted by pigeon-hole recesses. A careful inspection would have revealed that the slots did not extend the total depth of the box. In the back of the box lay the hidden radio. Most evenings Don would join Bob to listen to the BBC broadcasts. They would compare the stories of Allied and German broadcasts and knew that somewhere in between lay the truth.

The Germans were even more co-operative at Meiningen than they had been at Obermassfeld, supplying simple hand tools, (which they carefully checked every night), and providing raw material in the form of 4x4 planks of pine, and sometimes oak. From the Red Cross came supplies of leather, cotton batting and strips of flat metal. Don and his co-workers were permitted to take the metal across the street to the gas-works where a friendly blacksmith bent the strips to the required shapes and lengths — in return for the usual payment in cocoa and cigarettes.

The work soon became a routine: Don did the design work and the fittings aided by the doctors, and his two assistants, Farquhar and Perry, crafted the metal and leather into limbs to suit individual requirements. By the time of their release, they had made more than 350 legs and arms from the unpromising materials available. All amateurs in the job, they helped many soldiers and airmen to walk again. In so doing, the morale of the crippled prisoners was raised enormously. Many who had entered the camp despondent and unable to cope with the reality of their injuries were given new hope that they could walk again: more importantly, they realized that they would not be cut off from society by disability.

There was a constant turnover of prisoners. New ones entered the camps and others, too badly wounded to be of any further use as fighting men, were repatriated through the Red Cross. As they went back to Britain, the U.S. and Canada, they spread word of the diminutive Canadian who had given them the means to walk again. Even before his release, Don was becoming known back home.

Two of the repatriated Americans were Lieutenant Bert R. Shephard and Lieutenant Riba Whittle. Bert was a veteran U.S. pilot shot down during a raid over Berlin. His only recollection of the hit before losing consciousness was seeing his blown-off right leg hurtling earthward. Shephard had reason to be depressed when he arrived at Meiningen. A promising career as a professional baseball player with the Washington Senators had ended that day over Berlin. Don fitted him with a leg, thereby restoring Bert's mobility and his confidence as well. Shephard was repatriated and in 1945 and joined the Washington Senators. He pitched in a number of war-benefit games and one regular season game before taking on coaching responsibilities with the team.

Lieutenant Riba Whittle, a nurse with the U.S. Army Medical Services, was one of the very few American women taken prisoner in Germany. Riba was a flight nurse aboard an aerial ambulance which picked up patients from behind battle fronts. In early October 1944, after completing a scheduled pick-up of patients, the plane strayed off course and was shot down. The Germans were in a quandary about what to do with a female prisoner-of-war. They sent her to the prison hospital at Mieningen where her skills as a nurse would be useful. Whittle was repatriated on January 22, 1945. The publicity afforded to Don and his associates by Shephard, Whittle and others helped enormously in securing more supplies from the Red Cross, and greater co-operation from German officials who realized their defeat was inevitable.

In early March 1945 the Swedish exchange liner Gripsholm arrived in New York. Twenty-eight Allied Service men walked down the gang plank wearing an "Errey leg." Twenty-five were American officers, three were RCAF personnel from Alberta: Flying Officer J.N. Kenney, Nanton; Flying Officer Carl Rudyk, Edmonton; and W.O. D.C. Prowse, Tabor. Numerous British servicemen repatriated on the ship Arundel Castle arrived home on limbs fashioned in the makeshift workshop in Meiningen. They too became part of a growing cadre of Allied Service personnel attesting to the skill of the happy-go-lucky Canadian who remained a prisoner of Hitler's crumbling Third Reich.

$\mathcal{C}$HAPTER $\mathcal{T}$EN

With every passing day the Allies were drawing nearer to Germany, and morale in the camp was high. From the radio concealed in Bob Kost's room the prisoners received a constant stream of up-to-date information on the course of the war: Normandy, the breakthrough at Falaise, the liberation of Paris and Brussels, and the set-back at Arnhem. Only in late December, when the Germans broke through the lines in the Ardennes, did the prisoners spirits flag. But the Battle of the Bulge was the last dying gasp of the Wehrmacht in the West. As the Allies pushed on to the Rhine, the German guards in the hospital served as a barometer of their Army's fortunes. As the front crumbled they became more polite, and began to treat the prisoners almost as guests, rather than enemies of their country.

In the early spring of 1945 endless streams of soldiers and equipment passed through the town, motley convoys of anything that would move — trucks, private cars, bicycles, horse-drawn wagons, all carrying the defeated Germans further into the interior of their country. From the top floor of the hospital Don watched the trail of beaten men as they retreated from the Allies.

Then one morning he saw far in the distance the color of the uniforms turn from grey to olive-drab. Elements of Patton's Third U.S. Army were racing by in a pincer movement to cut off the retreating Germans. It wouldn't be long now before the prisoners would be freed. For several weeks, they had been living on a system of rationing, having decided to hoard the contents of their Red Cross parcels as the Reich crumbled. Under the circumstances they held little hope the Germans would continue to feed them.

On a bright spring morning the prisoners woke to find their prison deserted. The guards had cleared out, to follow the remnants of their army. The military had disappeared, but there were still civilians in the vicinity, and they began to mill around the perimeter of the camp. Necessity produced ingenuity; the gates were removed, the hinges reversed and then placed back in position so that they locked from the inside, to keep the civilians at a safe distance.

The following morning the guards returned and surrendered. The former prisoners of the Reich were now the custodians of their erstwhile jailers. The prisoners-turned-guards didn't lock up the German guards, but merely placed them in the rehabilitation huts until such time as the Allied army took responsibility for them. Meanwhile they waited.

There were still a few anxious moments. The main danger came, not from the Germans, but from the advancing allies. There were a few air raids on Meiningen, and some strafing by U.S. fighter-bombers, softening up the area in advance of their army. Don spent much of his time up in Bob's room, scanning the countryside with a pair of binoculars. Even though the buildings had large red crosses painted on their roofs, some of the prisoners had little confidence in the eyesight or accuracy of the fliers.

Eventually even the air activity ceased. There was still no sign of the Allied army. In boredom Don and Bob decided to go into the village, with Bob dressed in his RAF uniform and Don wearing most of a USAAF uniform. They found a couple of abandoned bicycles in the village and pedalled over to the British hospital, which was still full of bed patients. Bob decided to push on in a search for the Allied troops, while Don took a walk through the town. Outside the hospital a German officer approached him, saluted smartly, and declared that he wanted to surrender. With due gravity, Don accepted his surrender, his pistol, his sword, his medals, his armband, and then told him to buzz off. The officer, looking perplexed, did as he was told, leaving Don to meander in the deserted town. In company with a couple of orderlies from the hospital, he wandered into a bombed bank building. All over the floor were strewn bundles of useless Reichsmarks, French francs and English 5-pound notes. Not knowing whether or not they were forgeries, they gathered up several bundles and stuffed them in their pockets.

He got back to the camp to find it surrounded by civilians who pressed up to the wire to receive information from the inmates on the progress of the war. The POW's also received food which was passed through the wire to them. Like the guards, the civilians knew that the winds of fortune had changed direction.

On the morning of the 7th April 1945, Don and his comrades were aroused by the rumble of engines and the rattle of tank tracks. In the early sunlight they watched and cheered as the Shermans moved methodically around the perimeter and flattened the wire. The Allies had finally arrived, represented by the U.S. 11th armored division. The tanks were manned by black soldiers, who were something of a curiosity to the Germans. Most gratifying to the prisoners, the tankers brought in vast supplies of fresh white bread, canned butter, and cases of champagne; spoils of war which the regiment had liberated from some cellar the previous day. The prisoners gorged themselves on the unaccustomed luxuries.

The next column to appear was the U.S. army's supply echelon bringing more luxuries — soap, toothbrushes, socks, doughnuts — all things the POW's hadn't seen in years. Don threw away his tattered socks and changed into a new pair three times before the day ended, just to experience the joy of fresh cotton on his feet. They returned to their bunks that night a little groggy from the champagne and the rich food, but they slept the sleep of free men, knowing that they would soon return home.

Next day, the camp was visited by American medical personnel. The former POW's were all given a quick inspection, and most of them were pronounced fit to leave. Repatriation was due to begin in the next couple of days.

On the 11th April, 1945, Don boarded a USAAF Dakota destined for Paris. As the plane gained altitude the pilot dipped the port wing to give the ex-POWs a last glimpse of the camp. This was Don's first flight and the unsolicited good-will gesture of the pilot had mixed results. Although his eyes took in the miniature scene below, his mind and will concentrated on willing the aircraft to stay aloft. Eventually he relaxed and joined in the good-natured banter of soldiers heading home. Tall stories became taller with each retelling but no-one minded. Don looked forward to swapping tales with the Old Sweats from the Great War when he returned to Wallaceburg. His years as a POW held many bitter-sweet memories. As he enjoyed the outrageous stories being retold he knew that in time he too would recount only the sweet memories.

He was not one to spend much time thinking about the past, or what might have been. Perhaps the philosophy of living each moment as it came accounted for his survival since that September morning when he and Angus had swaggered off to war. Now, at least for him, the war was over; he had been lucky and had a future, no matter how uncertain. He would not waste precious years by dwelling on the past. The immediate concern was a long overdue date with Helen. The throbbing noise and sudden shudders of the Dakota as it sought a landing field near Paris could not erase his romantic thoughts.

The next morning Don was again airborne and in the late afternoon the Dakota touched down at an RAF station in the Midlands. He leapt from the aircraft and hurried off in search of the Orderly Room, If he were lucky he might catch an evening train to Edinburgh. However the inevitable red tape of military life proved unlucky.

"And just where do you think you are going, Corporal?", queried an RAF sergeant.

"The Orderly Room, sergeant", Don replied impatient at the delay, "to request leave".

The sergeant, in the soothing tone of all sergeants in every army, barked, "I have news for you Canada. There's a war on. Now get your arse over here and line up with the rest of the men". Don considered a few well-chosen words for a reply but resisted the temptation. He was home and back to army routine. Later he sent a telegram to Helen saying he was safe and would be with her soon.

During the week that followed Don was poked and prodded by a battery of medical zealots, who administered every vaccine or serum known, and in places rarely seen. All clothing was burned and every ex-POW deloused and issued a new uniform. A period of intensive and tedious debriefing followed. Each successive officer wanted Don to repeat, in detail, exactly what happened from the morning he had hit the beaches of Dieppe to the moment of his liberation. The repetition bored him as did the food. They were kept on a monotonous high protein diet restricted to eggs, milk and bread. But eventually the wisdom behind the diet became evident; Don, who arrived in England weighing 112 pounds, soon reached 120, well on his way to his normal weight of 140 pounds.

Debriefed and back to good health, Don set off once more for the Orderly Room in an effort to obtain leave. The Orderly clerk sympathized, but said he had no authority in the matter, and referred him to the Orderly Officer. The officer in turn passed him on to the Chief Administrative Officer, who, also sympathetic, said, "Rather bad luck, old boy, but there is nothing I can do. All the ex-POW Canadians are being transferred to a Canadian camp. Perhaps when you have settled in there you will be given leave". They were transferred to #1 Canadian Reception Depot near Aldershot. A second telegram was sent to Helen, again assuring her that he would be with her soon.

At the Reception Depot there were enlisted men from many Canadian Regiments. Most were in circumstances similar to Don's — their units had been decimated in battle and no longer existed. The regiments themselves continued to exist as new recruits replaced those killed, maimed or taken prisoner. The Essex Scottish had been rebuilt since the Dieppe disaster, and had become part of Canada's Third Division engaged in the liberation of Holland. As an ex-POW, Don could not join them on the Continent. The military brass believed that former prisoners of the Third Reich might be psychological risks as a result of their treatment in the camps. Don volunteered for service in the Pacific Theatre; fortunately for him he was never needed.

Days at the Reception Depot dragged. As a prisoner of the Germans for almost three years he had suffered the indignities of prison life, and had done his best to thwart the German war effort. He had also contributed in no small measure to the rehabilitation of his mates. Now he felt like a prisoner again. He had been liberated to a military bureaucracy whose endless red tape prevented him from seeing his fiancée. His patience was tried and was finally exhausted; if he couldn't find a way through the restrictions, he would ignore them.

Don mapped a strategy for 'escape'. He had talked his way out of six POW camps in Germany; getting out of his own camp should be easy. There were only two obstacles — money and a pass. Although most ex-POWs were owed years of back pay, it was not possible to obtain the full amount in one lump sum. The Paymaster Corps assumed, perhaps correctly, that most would have blown it all in one glorious evening of debauchery. The Corps wisely decided to disburse the money in a series of regular equal allotments. Don held them to their word. Each morning he paraded before the pay wicket and asked for a five-pound note, a modest request which was never refused. Within a week he had hoarded thirty pounds — enough for a train ticket to Edinburgh and a modest honeymoon.

Obtaining an evening pass was easy, but it required being back in camp the same night; failure to return risked the charge of "Absent Without Leave" (AWOL). Since Don had not seen his fiancee in three years he judged it a risk worth taking. As long as he returned to camp within thirty days he would only face the AWOL charge. Beyond thirty days, the charge would be desertion. That Don would avoid!

On the 24th April he sent a third telegram to Helen which read: "Find Bed. Arrive 7:30, 25th Waverley. Love, Don". That afternoon flashing his evening pass to the guards, he walked through the gates of

#1 Canadian Reception Depot. He would not return for four weeks.

At Cairns Memorial Chapel, Edinburgh, on 30th April 1945, Helen and Don were married. They managed a short and inexpensive honeymoon by staying with relatives in England, and were back in Edinburgh to celebrate V-E day on 8th May. The streets of the inner city were thronged with singing, dancing and roistering Scots. From behind the Waterloo pub, Don and several revellers gathered cardboard boxes and built a roaring bonfire in the middle of the street. Clasping hands they joined in singing "Auld Lang Syne" around the dying fire. A thousand war-weary Scots, singing the reunion song of their national poet, expressed the magic and euphoria of that special evening. There was not a dry eye anywhere. Six years of pent-up emotion burst forth in a wave of uncontrolled joy and laughter. Perhaps only those who had lived through the dark days of the war could ever understand the complete deliriousness of V-E day.

The celebrations dwindled as the week progressed. The Allies were still at war in the Pacific, and the city soon returned to its war-time routine. Don also had to return — to camp. He hated leaving Helen behind and the prospect of fourteen days confinement. A new plan was devised. Angus MacKenzie's older brother Donald was a sergeant in #9 Canadian Provost Corp stationed at Guildford. He called sergeant MacKenzie who acknowledged that Don's name was included on a lengthy list of AWOL Canadian servicemen. He told Don however not to worry. Hundreds of V-E day celebrants had been mysteriously afflicted by a sudden loss of memory as to the location of their camps. He arranged to meet Don and escorted him back to the Reception Depot. They collaborated on a plausible story explaining Don's absence. It worked. Don was let off with a reprimand and a few days of fatigue duty.

Shortly after his return a signal arrived with instructions for his repatriation to Canada. Don was ecstatic. He immediately phoned Helen with the good news. She was as excited by the news as Don, but felt a little apprehensive about going to the vast unknown land across the Atlantic, which she had often heard referred to as the "Frozen North". Apprehension gave way to a sense of adventure as Don explained in glowing terms the rugged, natural beauty of Canada. They proceeded with the paperwork necessary for Helen's emigration as a War-Bride. Don was scheduled to leave on a troop ship in June. Helen would follow when she received authorization from Canadian Immigration. She eventually sailed on the S. S. Mauretania with hundreds of other War-Brides, all of whom imagined themselves to be 'modern-day' pioneers off to settle the colonies. Fortunately for Helen, the land was as beautiful and life as rewarding as her husband had promised. For many other War-Brides the promises far exceeded the reality they encountered.

On the 14th June 1945, Don boarded the S. S. Volendam for Canada. After arriving at Halifax, the returnees were settled in a troop train destined for Montreal and connecting trains to towns and cities further west. For soldiers from Canada's West Coast, the train ride across the continent would take as much time as the Volendam's crossing of the Atlantic.

Don reached London, Ontario, on Sunday, June 24th. As he stepped down from the train he was immediately embraced by a pair of powerful arms. A proud and tearful Fred Errey had motored to London to greet his son. That evening at home in Wallaceburg, father and son talked into the early hours of the morning.

The following day, exhausted father and son cast ballots in the Federal election. This was the first time that Don was eligible to vote, and he knew where his vote would go. He had been among the troops who had given Prime Minister MacKenzie King the raspberry at Aldershot in 1941. Although the Liberals returned, Don had the satisfaction of seeing the Prime Minister go down to personal defeat in the riding of Prince Albert.

Satisfaction came also in a surprise reunion. The Washington Senators were in Detroit to play a three-game series with the Tigers. The Senators had arranged for Don to take part in a special pre-game ceremony. It was a childhood dream come true. He stood on the mound of Briggs Stadium beside Bert Shepherd, now a pitcher for the Senators, before a loudly cheering crowd. Don had the honour of tossing out the traditional first ball. After the game, Bert and Don sat quietly in the Visitors' dressing-room and swapped yarns for several hours. It had been only three months since Don's liberation from Stalag 9C-Meiningen and yet in that dressing-room it seemed a lifetime ago.

During that summer and fall the Canadian regiments in Europe began to come home. On 21st November the Essex Scottish returned to Windsor. The citizens of the city and surrounding area turned out in large numbers to welcome the boys home. A most enthusiastic welcomer was Don Errey clad in civilian attire. His discharge had been effective since 15th July.

Windsor was treated to an impressive home-coming parade by the regiment. As the Essex Scottish wheeled smartly out onto Ouellette Avenue, Don caught his first glimpse of the regiment since the Dieppe raid. The transformation of the regiment from the rag-tag assembly of eager civilians in 1939 to that of proud professional soldiers was complete. But, as they marched Don recognized few faces. Of the 553 members of the Essex Scottish who had raced across the barbed wired beaches of Dieppe on the early morning of August 19, 1942, only 52 managed to return to England that same evening.

One who would never return was Pte. Victor George Errey. Don's efforts to locate his brother had failed. In one last desperate attempt he had written to the Mayor of Dieppe. The Mayor diligently scrutinized the list of Canadian soldiers buried at the military cemetery but Vic's name was not among them. Reluctantly Don accepted that the Channel had claimed his missing brother.

As a final platoon of the regiment paraded past, Don heard the distinctive sound of the pipes. The band was playing the Regimental March. Instinctively he came to attention with thumbs pressing hard against the seams of his trousers. Tears formed in the corners of his eyes as the familiar strain of 'Highland Laddie' carried upon the wind. There were no grand phrases on his lips as he turned and slowly made his way through the milling crowd to a waiting car; those he left for the generals and politicians. For Don and thousands of other enlisted men, there was a more important task — rebuilding a life for themselves and their families.

Back cover photo: Don (left) with Bert   Shephard in the visitors dressing room, Briggs Stadium, Detroit. Summer 1945. On the right is the team trainer.